ROSEMARY SHRAGER'S ABSOLUTELY FOOLPROOF *CLASSIC* HOME COOKING

ROSEMARY SHRAGER'S ABSOLUTELY FOOLPROOF *CLASSIC* HOME COOKING

LYONS PRESS
Guilford, Connecticut

An imprint of Globe Pequot Press

CONTENTS

INTRODUCTION

I really feel I am one of those lucky people. I am doing work that I love and I have been privileged to meet wonderful chefs and to work with people who have helped me along the way. One of the most rewarding things about my work is that it gives me the opportunity to share with others my passion for food and cooking.

My love of food stems from my childhood. I was fortunate enough to be brought up knowing what good ingredients should taste like, in a family that liked to eat well. I call it the food gene. It was almost inevitable that I would have a career in food – though I actually started out studying interior design. This was very useful when I eventually started to work as a chef, as it meant I cared about how the dishes looked. I also studied sculpture and I love working with my hands. I'm a very tactile cook and I believe it's really important to handle the ingredients.

Because I didn't go to culinary school, I had to learn to cook on the job. This was an enjoyable thing to do but it was very tough at times, too. I wish I'd understood more when I first started cooking professionally. That's why I enjoy teaching so much. I want to share my hard-won knowledge, and I love seeing people's excitement and enthusiasm when they achieve their goals. One of the main things I hope to demonstrate when I teach is that cooking

is a lot of fun. I find it endlessly fascinating and constantly exciting. There is nothing better than seeing vegetables come into season or discovering a new flavor. One thing I have realized is that you never stop learning, and sometimes you find out the most interesting information from people and places you least expect.

If you want to learn to cook, remember that it's all about practice. You just have to keep trying. Making a dish once is never enough; you need to keep doing it until you really understand the technique. Some people are naturally talented cooks but, as with anything, at least 75 percent of their success is due to hard work – trying something over and over again until they get it right.

Mistakes happen, we all get it wrong at times, but what I aim to do in this book is help you minimize the mistakes and increase the foolproof factor. When I was learning to cook, I sometimes used to phone the chefs at Claridge's Hotel in London and ask them what I should do next. They were absolutely wonderful and always gave me good advice – even if it was only to start again. I hope that this book will prevent you having to do likewise if you need help! In it, I have tried to answer all the questions I have been asked during my time as a teacher – initially at my cooking school in Scotland, on the

Isle of Harris, and now at Swinton Park in North Yorkshire. One of the many reasons I love teaching is that it enables me to stay in touch with what aspiring cooks need to know.

Working in television has given me a much wider audience and I do believe that there is a huge place for food and cooking on television. The problem is, though, that there is never enough time to teach real techniques slowly and methodically. It sometimes seems that there is a whole generation who, through no fault of their own, have not had the opportunity to learn the basic techniques of cooking. That is where this book comes in. It aims to give you the confidence to tackle a complete set of cookery skills and to apply them to your everyday cooking. Some of the techniques might seem quite basic, such as a simple vinaigrette or a white sauce; others, like meringues and soufflés, sound more complex. However, it's important to mix the two together, because once you've learned to make a white sauce, for example, you can then use that knowledge to make a soufflé.

These classic techniques are used every single day in professional kitchens and are just as applicable at home. When you have mastered each technique and practiced it so you understand it thoroughly, you can use it as a base for your own recipes. The technique is there to teach you but the recipe itself is just a guideline. I have given plenty of variations on the main recipe in each chapter, so you will see that a recipe can be a starting point rather than an end in itself and you can create your own dishes too.

My book is designed to help you to build a great repertoire of home recipes to suit any occasion. You may think that terrines are rather old-fashioned or that soufflés are too difficult, but I believe that these are classic dishes that everyone should know how to cook. Terrines may look complicated, but they are incredibly easy to make, can be cooked in advance and are a great way to feed a lot of people. And what could be more delicious than a classic cheese soufflé? People are sometimes scared to try making soufflés and think they won't be able to do it, but this book provides foolproof steps for making them.

I hope that the way this book is set out will inspire you to work through it quite systematically, your confidence in your ability increasing with each chapter. Whatever your level of cookery knowledge, the tips and techniques will demystify the cooking process and help you on your way to better cooking – and better eating. It is a book for everybody, from young people leaving home to anyone, of whatever age, who simply wants to be a more knowledgeable cook. The most important thing to remember is not to be frightened of cooking – have fun with it!

NOTES ON THE RECIPES

■ All spoon measures are level unless otherwise stated.

■ All eggs are large unless otherwise stated. I much prefer to use good free-range eggs for the best color and flavor.

■ I like to use fine sea salt for dressings, salads and cold dishes and in bread making. Otherwise I use ordinary flaky sea salt.

■ Pepper should always be freshly ground. I use white pepper when I don't want to see the black grains in a dish but I do use black whenever I can, as I prefer the flavor.

■ I favor unsalted butter, as I like to add my own salt to a dish and I find I can control the flavor better in this way.

■ I recommend you seek out a good local flour if possible, as it makes all the difference to your baking.

■ It is very important to buy a good set of knives. For me, they are the tools of my trade. I use Wusthof knives, as they handle well and have a good weight.

SALADS
and
DRESSINGS

Salad ingredients are extremely useful to keep
in your fridge. They form the base of so many
instant meals or can be served with simple grilled
meat or fish. Once you have a winning formula
for salad dressings, you can stick with it and
adapt the flavorings as you like. Keep a jar
of vinaigrette or mayonnaise made up in the fridge
— you'll find it a godsend.

A mixed green salad dressed with vinaigrette is simplicity itself, but its success depends on careful seasoning and getting the balance of flavors right in the dressing. Choose leaves with a variety of textures. Try combining soft leaves, such as Webb, butterhead or lollo rosso, with crisp radicchio, Cos or Little Gem, and curly endive.

GREEN SALAD

with classic vinaigrette

To make the basic Classic Vinaigrette, follow steps 1 to 4

SERVES 4

FOR THE CLASSIC VINAIGRETTE:

1 teaspoon Dijon mustard

2½ teaspoons white wine vinegar

¼ cup extra virgin olive oil

½ cup sunflower oil

½ teaspoon sugar

fine sea salt and black pepper

FOR THE GREEN SALAD:

4 large handfuls of mixed salad leaves

a few sprigs of flat-leaf parsley

fine sea salt and black pepper

1 First make the vinaigrette. Put the mustard and vinegar in a small bowl.

2 Whisk with a small whisk or a fork until the mustard has dissolved.

3 Gradually pour in the two oils, whisking all the time.

4 Add the sugar, then season with salt and pepper to taste.

5 Wash the lettuce leaves thoroughly in cold water.

6 Drain well, wrap the leaves loosely in a tea towel and shake dry. Alternatively, you can use a salad spinner to dry the leaves.

7 Tear the lettuce into pieces and put them in a large bowl with the parsley sprigs. Season with a little salt and pepper.

8 Briefly whisk the vinaigrette again to emulsify it. Add 2½ tablespoons of vinaigrette to the salad.

9 Toss carefully, so the leaves don't reduce in volume too much. Taste a leaf and check the seasoning. Serve the salad with the rest of the vinaigrette on the side, so you can add a little more at the table if necessary.

TIPS AND IDEAS

■ I prefer to tear, rather than cut, most salad leaves as it gives a more attractive finish. If you have a tightly packed lettuce such as iceberg, Cos or Little Gem, however, you can cut it into shreds for a different look.

■ Lettuce bruises easily so treat it gently – I prefer to toss it with my hands, lifting and turning it over till all the leaves have a very light coating of the dressing.

■ Seasoning is crucial to a salad – you must taste all the way. I add 3 layers of seasoning: one to the leaves before dressing, one to the vinaigrette and then a final adjustment after dressing the salad.

■ The combination of sunflower and olive oil in this recipe makes a good all-purpose vinaigrette. Olive oil on its own can be rather intrusive but by all means use it if you want a stronger dressing.

■ Mustard thickens the vinaigrette slightly, besides adding flavor. If you don't like mustard, however, you can simply leave it out and increase the vinegar to 1 tablespoon.

■ Add interest to a plain green salad by tossing in any of the following: pine nuts, toasted almonds, thin strips of tomato, diced cooked smoked bacon, flowers such as nasturtiums, or herbs such as tarragon, mint, coriander and dill.

■ You can very easily make the vinaigrette in a jam jar. Just put in all the ingredients at once, screw the lid on and shake to emulsify.

■ To store salad leaves, wash them well, drain in a colander, then put them in a container in the fridge with a damp cloth over the top. They will keep for 2–3 days.

■ A plain vinaigrette such as this one will keep for at least a month in a sealed jar in the fridge. It's worth doubling the quantities so you always have some to hand. Don't store flavored vinaigrettes for more than a week, though, as the herbs and other flavorings can spoil.

vinaigrette variations

Herb Vinaigrette – put the ingredients for the Classic Vinaigrette in a blender with 1 tablespoon each of tarragon, coriander, parsley and mint and 1 chopped garlic clove. Blend together to make a dressing, then season to taste.

Asian Vinaigrette – omit the mustard from the Classic Vinaigrette and add 2½ teaspoons sugar, ½ finely chopped chile, 1 finely chopped garlic clove, 1 tablespoon finely chopped fresh ginger, 2 finely chopped spring onions, 2½ tablespoons chopped cilantro, the juice and grated zest of 1 lime and 2½ tablespoons sesame oil. Mix all the ingredients together well.

Citrus Vinaigrette – omit the vinegar and mustard from the Classic Vinaigrette and add the segments of 1 lemon and 1 orange and 1 tablespoon honey. Purée in a blender until smooth, then season well.

Dill Vinaigrette – omit the mustard from the Classic Vinaigrette. Put the remaining ingredients in a blender with a large bunch of dill and 1 tablespoon honey and purée. Season to taste. Wonderful with fish or chicken.

Garlic and Walnut Vinaigrette – make the Classic Vinaigrette, adding 5 tablespoons walnut oil, 4 very finely chopped garlic cloves, 2½ teaspoons lemon juice and, if you like, 6 chopped walnuts. Leave for as long as possible before serving so the vinaigrette becomes infused with the garlic, then strain. Excellent with meats and with vegetables that can take strong flavors, such as tomato and onion, beans, eggplant or zucchini.

For me, there is simply nothing as good as handmade mayonnaise, so thick you can stand a spoon up in it. It sounds daunting to make but in fact it just needs a little patience — the trick is to make sure your eggs are at room temperature and then add the oil to the yolks very slowly to prevent the mixture splitting. You can subtly alter the strength of your mayonnaise by using different oils, or produce countless variations on the basic recipe by adding herbs, spices and piquant ingredients such as capers and anchovies.

MAYONNAISE

MAKES ABOUT 1½ CUPS

2 egg yolks

1 teaspoon Dijon mustard

1¼ cups sunflower oil

¾ teaspoon fine sea salt

2½ tablespoons lemon juice, or to taste

1 Put a mixing bowl on a folded cloth to prevent it moving while you whisk. Add the egg yolks and mustard to the bowl.

2 Mix with a balloon whisk until the egg yolks and mustard are combined.

3 Pour the oil into a glass and stand a spoon in it.

4 Lift the spoon out of the glass and hold it straight over the yolks; this will ensure that you add just the right amount of oil drop by drop. Whisk constantly as you add the oil.

5 As the mixture becomes homogenous and the oil grips on to the protein in the egg, pour in the oil in a very slow, steady stream. Be careful, because this is where you might overdo it and the mayonnaise can split. If at any stage the mixture becomes too thick to whisk, add a drop of cold water or lemon juice.

6 When all the oil has been added and you have a smooth, glossy mayonnaise, season with the salt and add lemon juice to taste. If you're not using the mayonnaise straight away, cover and store in the fridge.

TIPS AND IDEAS

■ You can whisk in the oil with a hand-held electric beater, if you prefer. You can also make mayonnaise in a blender, briefly whizzing the yolks with the mustard and then slowly pouring in the oil through the hole in the lid. This gives a much thinner result than making it by hand, however.

■ If the mayonnaise starts to split, you can usually save it by whisking in a little water to bring it back together. If this doesn't work, put another egg yolk into a bowl and gradually add the curdled mixture to it drop by drop.

■ Mayonnaise made with sunflower oil provides a base for other flavorings, such as herbs and spices. You can also use extra virgin olive oil, or a mixture of olive and sunflower oil, for a more robustly flavored mayonnaise to serve with meat or fish.

■ Mayonnaise will keep, covered, in the fridge for about 3 days. Press a piece of cling film on to the surface to prevent oxidization.

SALADS AND DRESSINGS

mayonnaise variations

Saffron Mayonnaise – add a pinch of saffron strands to 2½ teaspoons boiling water and leave to infuse for 10 minutes or until the water is cold. Gradually stir into the Mayonnaise.

Rouille – follow the recipe on pages 16–17, replacing the sunflower oil with olive oil. Add 2 crushed garlic cloves, ½ teaspoon cayenne pepper and 1 teaspoon paprika, then season with more salt. This is fantastic with shellfish, spread on top of a crouton to serve with fish soup, or just served as a dip for bread.

Dill Mayonnaise – this is very good with cured fish or meats. Follow the recipe on pages 16–17, doubling the amount of mustard and adding a large bunch of chopped dill (be careful not to chop it too much, as dill is a very watery herb) and 2½ teaspoons sugar.

Tartar Sauce – this is a classic accompaniment to fried fish but also goes well with grilled fish or cooked chicken and can be used as a dip. Add to the Mayonnaise 1 teaspoon finely chopped shallot, 2½ teaspoons finely chopped drained capers, 2½ teaspoons runny honey, 1 tablespoon each of finely chopped chives and parsley and 2½ teaspoons lemon juice.

Remoulade Mayonnaise – this is very versatile and goes with anything. Stir into the Mayonnaise 2½ teaspoons finely chopped drained capers, 2½ teaspoons finely chopped gherkins, 1 finely chopped anchovy fillet, 2½ teaspoons Dijon mustard, 1 tablespoon each of finely chopped tarragon and parsley and some black pepper.

CELERIAC AND APPLE SALAD

This is an ideal salad for the depths of winter. Serve as an accompaniment to cold meats.

Serves 4

18 ounces celeriac

2 tart eating apples, preferably Granny Smith

juice of 2 lemons

2½ tablespoons Mayonnaise
(see pages 16–17)

2½ tablespoons olive oil

2½ tablespoons chopped chives

2½ tablespoons finely chopped parsley

2 shallots, finely chopped

2 gherkins, finely chopped

fine sea salt and black pepper

1 Peel the celeriac and cut it into 1/4-inch cubes. Cook in boiling salted water for 1–2 minutes or until just tender, then drain, refresh under cold running water and leave to cool completely.

2 Peel and core the apples and cut them into 1/4-inch cubes. Mix with the lemon juice, then add the celeriac and all the remaining ingredients. Stir together gently and season with salt and pepper to taste. Refrigerate until required.

CHICKEN SALAD WITH MANGO AND ALMONDS

I got the idea for this from a Chinese cookbook years ago. Fruit and lean white meat make a wonderfully nutritious combination.

Serves 4

3 skinless, boneless chicken breasts

olive oil

3.5 ounces flaked almonds

1 mango, peeled and diced

2½ tablespoons finely chopped chives, plus extra to garnish

juice of 1 lime

2 handfuls of arugula

fine sea salt and black pepper

For the dressing:

½ cup Mayonnaise (see pages 16–17)

¼ cup crème fraîche

½ teaspoon garam masala

1 teaspoon runny honey

1 Cut each chicken breast lengthways into 3 and toss with a little oil until well coated. Season with salt and pepper. Place a frying pan over a medium heat, drizzle in a little oil and fry the chicken quickly, until cooked through but not browned. Transfer to a colander to drain and leave to cool. Now roughly shred the chicken.

2 Mix the mayonnaise with the crème fraîche, garam masala and honey. Put the chicken pieces into a bowl and add the flaked almonds, mango, chives, lime juice and the dressing. Mix carefully.

3 Divide the arugula between 4 serving plates. Pile the chicken mixture on top, sprinkle with chives and serve.

SHRIMP, CELERY, FENNEL AND OLIVE SALAD

I love the combination of shrimp and olives. It's something you wouldn't expect to work but it just does. The trick here is to use very good olive oil and to add it to the shrimp when they're still slightly warm. A great salad to make in advance as a starter.

Serves 4

20 large raw shrimp, shelled

1 small fennel bulb, sliced very thinly, preferably on a mandoline

1 small celery heart

8 black olives, stoned

5 tablespoons olive oil

juice of 1 lemon

fine sea salt and black pepper

a little watercress, to garnish

1 Remove the black thread that runs down the back of each shrimp with the point of a knife. Put the shrimp in a steamer and steam for 2–3 minutes, until they turn pink. Cool slightly and then cut the shrimp horizontally in half. Put them in a large bowl.

2 Cook the fennel in boiling salted water for 3 minutes or until tender, then drain, refresh under cold running water and drain again.

3 Strip the celery of its strings and cut the stalks into very thin batons. Cut the olives into small strips. Add these to the shrimp with the fennel, oil and lemon juice and toss thoroughly. Just before serving, season well with salt and pepper and sprinkle with watercress.

SALADE NIÇOISE

A classic dish. Season every element separately for the best flavor, rather than just seasoning the salad at the end.

Serves 4

14-ounce tuna fillet

16 baby new potatoes, scrubbed

3.5 ounces green beans

4 vine-ripened tomatoes

2 baby Little Gem lettuces

5–7 tablespoons Classic Vinaigrette
(see pages 12–13)

a bunch of basil

6 anchovy fillets (use marinated fresh ones),
cut lengthways in half

12 black olives, pitted

2 eggs, hard-boiled (see page 72) and cut
into quarters

fine sea salt and black pepper

a few flat-leaf parsley leaves, to garnish

1 Put the tuna into the freezer for 2 hours to make it easier to slice.

2 Cook the potatoes in boiling salted water until just tender, then drain well and set aside. Trim the beans and cook in boiling salted water for just 2 minutes. Drain, refresh under cold water and set aside.

3 Cut the tomatoes into quarters or, if they are large, into 6. Separate the lettuce leaves but keep them whole. Using a large, sharp knife, slice the tuna as thinly as possibly.

4 Cut the potatoes into halves or quarters if large. Put them in a large bowl with the tomatoes and beans and toss in 4 tablespoons of the vinaigrette. Season well with salt and pepper. Now carefully toss in the basil leaves, sliced tuna, anchovy fillets and black olives, adding a little more vinaigrette if necessary. Put into a clean bowl and season again if necessary. Now put in the eggs and, to look pretty, sprinkle a few leaves of parsley over.

COUSCOUS SALAD WITH LEMON

This is delicious as a salad and can also be eaten warm. Be careful not to soak the couscous for too long or it will be overly fluffy. Cut the herbs as finely as you can for the best flavor.

Serves 6

9 ounces couscous

1 chile, very finely chopped

grated zest of 1 lemon

2 garlic cloves, very finely chopped

4 tomatoes, skinned, deseeded and diced (see
page 135)

2½ teaspoons freshly ground black pepper

2½ tablespoons very finely chopped parsley

2½ tablespoons very finely chopped mint

3½ tablespoons very finely chopped chives

1 cup chicken stock (see pages 30–31)

For the vinaigrette:

¼ cup olive oil

1 tablespoon lemon juice

2½ teaspoons honey

fine sea salt and black pepper

1 Put the couscous into a bowl, add all the ingredients except the stock and stir well. Bring the stock to a boil and pour it over the couscous mixture. Stir, cover with plastic wrap and then leave to stand for about 10 minutes. Meanwhile, whisk together all the ingredients for the vinaigrette.

2 Remove the plastic wrap from the couscous and stir gently with a fork to fluff it up. Now stir in the vinaigrette to taste.

CANNELLINI BEANS WITH TOMATOES AND GARLIC

This makes a great salad with a barbecue and is an excellent vegetarian dish.

Serves 4–6

9 ounces dried cannellini beans, soaked in cold water overnight

1 onion, unpeeled but quartered

2 bay leaves

5 tablespoons olive oil

4 garlic cloves, finely chopped

14 ounces tomatoes, skinned, deseeded and chopped (see page 135)

a handful of sage leaves, chopped

¼ cup extra virgin olive oil

5 tablespoons finely chopped parsley

sea salt and black pepper

1 Place the beans, onion and bay leaves in a pan and cover generously with cold water. Bring to a boil, then reduce the heat and simmer for about 1 hour, until the beans are tender. Drain well, discarding the onion and bay leaves. Set the beans aside.

2 Heat the olive oil in a shallow pan, add the garlic and cook for a minute, then add the tomatoes and cook until any juices have evaporated. Stir in the beans and sage, season to taste with salt and pepper and cook gently for 20 minutes. Add the extra virgin olive oil, mix well and season to taste. Sprinkle with the parsley and serve warm or cold.

CAESAR SALAD WITH CHICKEN

Marinated fresh anchovies in oil are best for this, although canned anchovies will be fine.

Serves 4

1 tablespoon heavy cream or yogurt

juice of 1½ lemons

½ quantity of Mayonnaise (see pages 16–17)

4 small skinless, boneless chicken breasts

2½ tablespoons extra virgin olive oil

1 Cos lettuce

12 anchovies in oil, drained, cut lengthways in half if large

1.5 ounces Parmesan cheese, cut into shavings with a vegetable peeler

4 handfuls of croutons (see page 38)

2½ tablespoons roughly chopped flat-leaf parsley

sea salt and black pepper

1 Stir the cream or yogurt and the juice of 1/2 lemon into the mayonnaise and set aside.

2 Mix the chicken breasts with the juice of the remaining lemon and the olive oil, then season with salt and pepper. Leave a ridged grill pan over a high heat until it is very hot, put the chicken breasts on it and turn the heat down to medium. Leave the chicken breasts undisturbed for 4 minutes so you achieve nice clean lines underneath. Turn them over and cook the other side for 4 minutes or until the chicken is completely cooked through; the juices should run clear when it is pierced with a knife. Remove from the grill and leave to rest for 10 minutes while you make the salad.

3 Tear the Cos lettuce into pieces and put them into a bowl. Toss with a little of the dressing – just enough to coat the leaves lightly – then gently mix in the anchovies, shaved Parmesan, croutons and most of the parsley. Divide between 4 serving plates. Cut the chicken into long pieces, lay them on top of the salad and drizzle the remaining mayonnaise over. Sprinkle with the remaining parsley, season with black pepper and serve.

HALIBUT CEVICHE WITH TOMATO AND AVOCADO SALSA

This fresh and zingy dish has Spanish origins but is now associated with South America and Central America. It can be prepared several hours in advance. I find cooking in advance an absolute joy, as you can relax when it is time to serve.

Serves 4

1¼-pound halibut fillet, skinned, any bones removed

juice of 3 limes

juice of 1 lemon

1 bird's eye chile, finely chopped

2 large shallots, finely sliced

2 garlic cloves, finely chopped

4 green onions, finely chopped

2½ tablespoons finely chopped cilantro

5 tablespoons extra virgin olive oil

fine sea salt and black pepper

For the tomato and avocado salsa:

2 large, vine-ripened tomatoes, skinned, deseeded and finely diced (see page 135)

1 avocado, peeled, pitted and finely diced

juice of 1 lemon

1 tablespoon finely chopped chives

1 Cut the halibut into 3/4-inch chunks and put them into a bowl. Add the lime and lemon juice and mix gently. Add the chopped chile and sliced shallots, mix again, then cover and leave for 3–4 hours.

2 To make the salsa, mix all the ingredients together in a bowl. Season with salt and pepper just before serving, so that the salt does not draw out the liquid from the tomatoes.

3 Drain the halibut, add the garlic, green onions, cilantro and oil and mix together gently. Season well with salt and pepper and serve with the salsa.

HOT-SMOKED SALMON WITH CRÈME FRAÎCHE AND SPINACH

This is such an easy starter or main dish if you haven't got much time.

Serves 4 as a starter or a light main course

14 ounces hot-smoked salmon

4 handfuls of baby spinach

¾ cup crème fraîche

2½ tablespoons olive oil

2½ teaspoons white wine vinegar

fine sea salt and black pepper

1 tablespoon pink peppercorns (optional), to garnish

Start by gently flaking the hot-smoked salmon. Wash and dry the spinach. Mix the crème fraîche, olive oil, vinegar, black pepper and a little salt. Put a handful of spinach on each plate, cover with salmon and top with the sauce. Garnish with pink peppercorns, if you like.

DUCK CARPACCIO SALAD WITH ANCHOVY DRESSING

The reason for not marinating the duck for too long is because the lemon will start cooking the duck breast. The anchovy really enhances the duck.

Serves 4

½ cup white wine

1 tablespoon olive oil

1 tablespoon finely chopped shallot

5 teaspoons lemon juice

2 sprigs of thyme

2 duck breasts, skinned

9 ounces mixed baby salad leaves

fine sea salt and black pepper

For the anchovy dressing:

2 anchovy fillets in oil, finely chopped

2½ tablespoons lemon juice

1 tablespoon white wine vinegar

7 tablespoons extra virgin olive oil

1 tablespoon chopped chives

1 Mix together the wine, oil, shallot, lemon juice, thyme and some salt and pepper, pour over the duck breasts and leave to marinate for about 20 minutes. Drain and dry them, then fry over a high heat for 30 seconds on each side in a non-stick frying pan, until browned on the outside but still raw inside. Remove from the heat and leave to rest for at least 5 minutes.

2 Meanwhile, whisk all the dressing ingredients together, then taste and adjust the seasoning. Toss the salad leaves with a little of the dressing and divide them between 4 serving plates. Carve the duck in thin slices and arrange on the salad. Drizzle over a little more dressing and serve.

CARROT SALAD WITH ORANGE AND OREGANO

A tantalizingly fresh winter or summer salad.

Serves 4

14 ounces carrots, peeled and cut into matchsticks

5 tablespoons olive oil

grated zest and juice of 1 orange

3½ tablespoons chopped oregano

1 tablespoon chopped parsley

fine sea salt and black pepper

Cook the carrots in boiling salted water for 1 minute, then drain and refresh under cold running water. Drain again, pat dry with kichen paper and mix with the olive oil and orange juice. Toss with the rest of the ingredients, then adjust the seasoning if necessary.

GREEN BEANS WITH LEMON VINAIGRETTE

It's best to add the oil when the beans are still warm, so it really brings out their flavor.

Serves 4

18 ounces green beans

5 tablespoons olive oil

juice of 1 lemon

fine sea salt and black pepper

First trim the beans – do not buy ready-trimmed ones, as they usually taste stale. Cook the beans in boiling salted water till just tender, then drain thoroughly. Dry the beans, then put them in a serving dish and toss with the oil, lemon juice and some salt and plenty of pepper. Serve cold.

POTATO AND CABBAGE WITH SAFFRON MAYONNAISE

This is very good served with grilled chicken or fish.

Serves 4 generously

2¼ pounds waxy potatoes, peeled

1 medium Savoy cabbage

6 green onions, finely chopped

2½ tablespoons finely chopped chives

For the saffron mayonnaise:

a pinch of saffron strands, steeped in 2½ teaspoons boiling water

½ quantity of Mayonnaise (see pages 16–17)

fine sea salt and black pepper

1 Cook the potatoes in boiling salted water until tender, then drain well.

2 Cut the central stalk out of the cabbage and remove all the core. Roll up the leaves and cut them into very fine strips. Cut the cooked potatoes into 1/2-inch dice and put them in a bowl with the cabbage. Add the green onions and chives.

3 Mix the saffron liquid into the mayonnaise and season well to taste. Toss with the vegetables, being careful not to overload them with mayonnaise. Adjust the seasoning and serve straight away.

STOCKS
and
SOUPS

Stock is easy to make at home and it will taste so much better than the ones you can buy. It's also economical, using just bones and a few aromatics, such as onion, carrot, celery and herbs. Soups, too, always taste nicer when you make them yourself, and you can use whatever is in season. But be sure to season them well — you will be surprised how much seasoning a soup needs.

Chicken stock is the most useful and versatile of all, and a really good home-made one is essential for this soup. Once you've got your stock, it's very quick to make the little dumplings, and they cook in the broth in a matter of minutes.

CHICKEN BROTH

with Asian chicken and pork dumplings

To make the basic chicken stock, follow steps 1 to 8

SERVES 4

2½ tablespoons mirin (Japanese rice wine)

1 tablespoon soy sauce, or to taste

FOR THE CHICKEN STOCK (MAKES ABOUT 2 QUARTS):

1 chicken, cut into pieces, or some raw carcasses with the trimmings, or chicken portions such as wings – you will need 3½–4½ pounds total

1 large onion, roughly chopped

1 large carrot, roughly chopped

1 large celery stick, roughly chopped

2 sprigs of parsley

2 sprigs of thyme

2 bay leaves

1 teaspoon black peppercorns

2–2½ quarts of water

FOR THE DUMPLINGS:

3.5 ounces chicken breast

3.5 ounces finely ground pork

1 teaspoon cornstarch

2 green onions, finely chopped

2½ tablespoons finely chopped parsley

2 garlic cloves, finely chopped

1 tablespoon finely chopped fresh ginger

5 tablespoons fresh breadcrumbs

1 egg yolk

1 tablespoon soy sauce

sea salt and black pepper

1 Chop the chicken or chicken carcass into pieces.

2 Put the chicken pieces into a large saucepan.

3 Add the vegetables, herbs and black peppercorns.

4 Add enough cold water just to cover.

5 Bring to a boil.

6 Reduce the heat and simmer very gently, uncovered, for about 1½ hours. Skim any froth from the surface occasionally but do not stir.

7 Strain the stock through a fine sieve into a bowl – it's easier to strain if you remove any large bones with tongs first.

8 Leave to cool, then chill – any fat will rise to the surface and solidify and can be easily removed. Refrigerate if not using immediately.

9 Put the chicken breast into a food processor.

10 Process briefly, so the chicken is not too puréed.

11 Transfer the chicken to a bowl; add all the remaining ingredients for the dumplings.

12 Mix well. Then chill the dumpling mixture for 20 minutes.

13 Lightly shape the mixture into small balls, about ¾ inch in diameter, dampening your hands slightly to prevent sticking.

14 You can cook one ball to check the seasoning, either by frying it in a little oil or poaching it in stock or water. If necessary, adjust the seasoning.

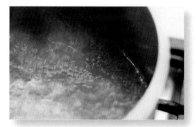

15 Bring the stock to a simmer in a large pan and taste it; if the flavour isn't strong enough, boil the stock until it has reduced slightly.

16 Stir in the mirin and soy sauce.

17 Add the dumplings to the stock.

18 Poach very gently for 4–6 minutes – the bubbles should be barely breaking the surface of the liquid. When the dumplings are cooked through, serve immediately, with the broth.

TIPS AND IDEAS

■ Choose your aromatics to suit the stock – for example, fennel or a strip of orange peel for fish, a couple of cloves for beef. Only add a little of each aromatic; the flavor should be subtle rather than dominant.

■ You can use leek tops, herb stalks and fennel tops for stocks – all the bits you would otherwise throw away. Practically any vegetable can be added to stock but avoid starchy ones, such as potatoes, as they absorb the flavor into themselves.

■ There is no need to peel carrots and onions for stock; just wash them, and remove the roots from the onions.

■ There is no need to season stocks. I like to be in control of my seasoning when cooking, and starting with an unseasoned stock means I can then decide how much flavor to add.

■ To make a darker chicken stock, roast the bones in a hot oven for an hour before you start (but be careful not to burn them). This caramelization gives color and flavor and also removes the fat from the bones.

■ Leftover cooked chicken carcasses can also be used to make stocks but I find they work better for soups than sauces. This is also a good way of using up the turkey carcass – add 1/2 bottle of white wine with all the other ingredients.

■ Always add cold water rather than hot to the bones – it makes a better, clearer stock.

■ Stock must simmer very gently, with the bubbles barely breaking the surface. If the stock boils vigorously it will become cloudy.

■ For a clear stock, skimming is important – use a large spoon to remove scum and impurities from the surface, but do not stir as you want to create a lovely, clear stock and stirring will make it cloudy.

■ After straining your stock, it's worth tasting it to see if it is strong enough. If you want to intensify the flavor, boil it until it has reduced and concentrated to your liking.

■ Chicken stock will keep in the fridge for 4 days or can be frozen. I like to store it in water bottles or plastic bags.

BEEF STOCK

When you buy a joint of beef, ask your butcher to give you the bones so you can make a lovely stock. It takes time to cook but very little of your time to make. You can omit the wine, if you like, and then it will cost just pennies.

Makes about 1 quart

4½ pounds beef bones or veal bones

2 large onions, peeled and quartered

½ bottle of red wine

2 carrots, roughly chopped

2 bay leaves

4 garlic cloves, roughly chopped

2 sprigs of thyme or a few parsley stalks

2½ teaspoons black peppercorns

1 Put the bones and onions in a large roasting pan and put it in an oven preheated to 425°F for about 1 hour until they're brown all over – this length of time gives a good color and flavor to the stock. Remove everything from the roasting pan and put it into a large saucepan. Pour off the fat from the roasting tin, place the pan on the stovetop and pour in the red wine. Bring to a boil, stirring and scraping the bottom of the pan with a wooden spoon to deglaze it. Pour this into the saucepan with the bones. Add enough cold water just to cover the bones; you do not want to drown them or the flavor will be watery. Add all the remaining ingredients to the saucepan. Bring to a boil, then reduce the heat to a very low simmer. Cook for about 3 hours, regularly skimming off any scum from the surface and topping up with a little more water if necessary.

2 Strain the stock through a fine sieve and leave to cool. Keep in the fridge for up to 4 days and discard the fat from the top before using.

3 You can take this recipe a step further and reduce the stock for a more intense and stronger flavor. This will reduce the volume.

GAME STOCK

Game stock makes the most wonderful soup. I like to add a pig's foot to it, because it makes it slightly more gelatinous and gives a deeper flavor, but you can omit it if necessary.

Makes about 1⅓ quarts

6½ pounds raw game bones and/or carcasses, chopped

1 pig's foot, chopped (optional)

½ bottle of red wine

1 large onion, grated

2 carrots, roughly chopped

2 celery sticks, roughly chopped

2½ teaspoons black peppercorns

1 tablespoon juniper berries

2 bay leaves

a few sprigs of thyme

1 First put the bones and the pig's foot, if using, into a roasting pan, place in an oven preheated to 425°F and roast for about 30 minutes, until brown. Remove the bones from the roasting pan and put them into a large saucepan. Pour off any fat from the roasting pan, place the pan on the stovetop and pour in the red wine. Bring to a boil, stirring and scraping the bottom of the pan with a wooden spoon to deglaze it. Pour this into the saucepan with the bones. Add enough cold water just to cover the bones, then add all the remaining ingredients to the saucepan. Bring to a boil then reduce the heat to a very low simmer. Cook for about 2 hours, skimming off any scum from the surface and topping up with a little more water if necessary.

2 Strain the stock through a fine sieve and leave to cool. Store in the fridge for up to 4 days and discard the fat from the top before using.

FISH STOCK

The important thing about making stock from fish bones, as opposed to meat, is that it mustn't be cooked too long or it will go cloudy. Use only white fish bones, not oily salmon or trout bones.

Makes about 1½ quarts

4½ pounds cleaned bones, skins, heads, tails and fins of white fish

½ fennel bulb, roughly chopped

1 leek, roughly chopped

1 onion, roughly chopped

6 sprigs of parsley

2½ teaspoons peppercorns

2 bay leaves

½ bottle of white wine

1 Make sure all the fish bones have been well cleaned and that the livers and any blood have been removed. Put all the ingredients in a saucepan, add enough water just to cover and bring slowly to a boil. Reduce the heat, skim any scum from the surface and simmer very gently for 30 minutes, skimming again occasionally.

2 Strain the stock through a fine sieve and leave to cool. Keep in the fridge for only a couple of days, or freeze.

VEGETABLE STOCK

This is such an easy thing to make. I tend to use leftover vegetables and you can just toss them in the pot and boil them up.

Makes about 1¾–2 quarts

2 onions, roughly chopped

2 leeks, roughly chopped

2 celery sticks, roughly chopped

2 garlic cloves, roughly chopped

2 bay leaves

2 lemongrass stalks

2 sprigs each of tarragon and parsley

2½ teaspoons black peppercorns

½ bottle of white wine

1½ quarts water

Put all the ingredients except the water into a large saucepan and bring to a boil. Simmer for 5 minutes, then add the water and bring back to the boil. Reduce the heat and simmer for 30 minutes, stirring and skimming occasionally. Leave to cool and then strain through a fine sieve. Keep in the fridge for a couple of days, or freeze.

VICHYSSOISE

This leek and potato soup is traditionally served cold but I also love it hot, which is what I have suggested here. Ideally the weight of the peeled potatoes and leeks should be equal, so the quantity of leeks you need to start off with will depend on whether you buy ones that have had their green tops trimmed off.

Serves 6

about 16 ounces potatoes, peeled

18–26 ounces leeks, trimmed and green parts removed

4 tablespoons unsalted butter

2 garlic cloves, finely chopped

2½ cups chicken stock (see pages 30–31) – plus a little more if necessary

1¼ cups milk

⅔ cup heavy cream

sea salt and black pepper

1 tablespoon finely chopped chives, to garnish

1 Cut the potatoes into small dice. Cut up the leeks into small pieces. Melt the butter in a large pan, add the garlic and leeks and cook gently for about 5 minutes, until softened. Now add the potatoes, stock and milk, bring to a boil and simmer for 40 minutes.

2 Remove the soup from the heat and allow to cool for 10 minutes, then purée in a blender, in batches. Pour back into the pan and reheat gently, adding a little more stock if the soup is too thick. Season well with salt and pepper, stir in the cream and serve the soup garnished with the chives.

SUMMER MINESTRONE WITH PESTO

This is the perfect summer soup. On a very hot day, try serving it cold for a refreshing starter.

Serves 4

12 asparagus spears

5 tablespoons olive oil, plus extra for drizzling

4 large green onions, sliced

9 ounces new potatoes, scraped and cut into small dice

18 ounces peas in their pods, shelled (or 5 ounces frozen peas)

4 ounces green beans, trimmed, then cut into short lengths

about 1 quart vegetable stock (see page 35)

2¼ pounds fava beans in their pods, shelled

1 quantity of Pesto (see page 138)

2½ tablespoons chopped mint

2½ tablespoons torn basil

sea salt and black pepper

1 Trim the asparagus by breaking off the lower woody part of each stem. Cut the stems into short lengths, reserving the tips. Set aside.

2 Heat the olive oil in a large pan, add the green onions and cook gently until softened. Add the potatoes, peas, green beans and asparagus stalks (but not the tips) and cook, stirring, for 2 minutes. Add enough vegetable stock to cover and then bring to a boil. Simmer for 10 minutes or until the potatoes are tender.

3 Cook the fava beans in boiling water for 1 minute, until tender, then drain and slip off the thin green skins. Boil the asparagus tips for 1 minute, then drain and add them to the soup with the fava beans. Season to taste with salt and pepper, remove from the heat and stir in the pesto. Adjust the seasoning if necessary, scatter with the chopped mint and basil, then drizzle with olive oil before serving.

TOMATO SOUP WITH BASIL AND CROUTONS

This is one of the nicest things you can make when you have an abundance of tomatoes in the summer and they are good and ripe.

Serves 6

2½ tablespoons olive oil

2 shallots, finely chopped

6 garlic cloves, finely chopped

1 large carrot, finely chopped

4½ pounds ripe tomatoes, cut into quarters

2½ tablespoons tomato paste

4 sprigs of parsley, roughly chopped

1¼ quarts chicken stock (see pages 30–31)

1 teaspoon superfine sugar

20 basil leaves, finely chopped

sea salt and black pepper

For the croutons:

4 thick slices of white bread

olive oil

1 Heat the oil in a large heavy-bottomed saucepan, add the shallots, garlic and carrot and cook gently until softened but not colored. Now add the chopped tomatoes, tomato purée and parsley and stir well. Add the stock and gently simmer for 30 minutes without a lid. Remove from the heat and allow to cool for about 20 minutes. Put the stock into a blender, in batches, and whiz until smooth. Pour through a sieve to remove the seeds. Pour into a clean pan, reheat gently, add the sugar and season well with salt and pepper. Stir in the basil.

2 To make the croutons, cut the bread into 1/3-inch dice and spread them out in a baking pan. Drizzle with olive oil, put them into an oven preheated to 300°F and cook for about 30 minutes, until golden, shaking the pan a few times. Serve the soup with the croutons scattered on top.

SPINACH AND WATERCRESS SOUP

A fantastically quick soup to make, with a lovely vibrant color. Be sure to season it very well.

Serves 4

4 tablespoons unsalted butter

2 shallots, finely chopped

16 ounces fresh spinach

9 ounces watercress, with stalks

2 cups chicken stock (see pages 30–31)

⅔ cup heavy cream

sea salt and black pepper

8 chives, finely chopped, to garnish

1 Melt the butter in a large saucepan, add the shallots and cook gently until softened. Stir in the spinach and watercress and cook over a low heat until wilted. Pour in the chicken stock, bring to a boil, then reduce the heat and simmer for 5 minutes. Cool slightly, then purée in a blender – do this in batches if necessary.

2 Pour the soup into a clean pan, reheat gently and season to taste with salt and pepper. Swirl in the cream and serve garnished with the chopped chives.

MUSSEL AND COCONUT SOUP

I just adore this soup, and could eat it all the time. It's quite rich because of the coconut milk, but well worth the effort.

Serves 4

4½ pounds mussels

1 tablespoon olive oil

2 garlic cloves, chopped

leaves from 2 sprigs of thyme

¾ cup fish stock (see page 35) or chicken stock (see pages 30–31)

13.5-ounce can of coconut milk

1 lemongrass stalk, halved lengthwise

1 red bird's eye chile, deseeded and thinly sliced

2 green onions, thinly sliced

sea salt and black pepper

chopped cilantro, to garnish

1 Scrub the mussels under cold running water, pulling out and discarding the 'beards'. Discard any open mussels that don't close when tapped lightly on the work surface.

2 Put the olive oil, garlic, thyme, mussels and stock in a large pan, cover the pan with a lid and place over a medium heat. Let the mussels steam for 4–5 minutes, until they are fully opened, shaking the pan occasionally. Scoop out the mussels with a slotted spoon, discarding any that haven't opened, and place in a bowl. Strain the cooking liquid through a fine sieve into a large clean plan and boil until reduced by half. Add the coconut milk, lemongrass, chile, green onions and some seasoning and simmer for a couple of minutes.

3 Divide the mussels between 4 bowls. Remove the lemongrass from the pan. Pour the soup over the mussels, sprinkle with chopped cilantro and serve.

CHESTNUT AND PARSNIP SOUP

This is a gorgeous winter soup, and just right for serving at Christmas.

Serves 6

3 tablespoons unsalted butter

3.5 ounces leeks (white part only), finely chopped

1 small onion, finely chopped

a sprig of thyme

1 garlic clove, finely chopped

2 bay leaves

11 ounces cooked chestnuts, chopped (canned or vacuum-packed chestnuts are fine)

12 ounces parsnips, finely chopped

3 cups chicken stock (see pages 30–31)

¾ cup heavy cream

sea salt and black pepper

1 Heat the butter in a saucepan, add the leeks and onion and cook gently until softened. Add the thyme, garlic and bay leaves and cook for 5 minutes. Stir in the chestnuts and cook for 2 minutes, then add the parsnips and cook for 5 minutes longer. Pour in the chicken stock, bring to a boil, then reduce the heat and simmer for 45 minutes.

2 Cool the soup slightly, then blend in a blender in batches. Reheat gently. Add the heavy cream and season well with salt and pepper.

FRENCH ONION SOUP

There's nothing better on a winter's night than this classic soup. Sometimes I put a puff pastry crust on top instead of croutons, brush it with egg and put it in a hot oven for about 20 minutes, until golden and burnished.

Serves 4

4 tablespoons unsalted butter

3½ tablespoons extra virgin olive oil

1¾ pounds Spanish onions, sliced

2½ tablespoons sugar

2½ tablespoons all-purpose flour

1½ quarts beef stock (see page 34)

¼ cup brandy (optional)

8 rounds of day-old French bread, lightly toasted

9½ tablespoons finely grated Gruyère cheese

sea salt and black pepper

1 Heat the butter and oil in a large pan, add the onions and cook over a low heat until very soft. This will take up to 30 minutes. Sprinkle in the sugar and continue cooking until the onions are golden brown. Stir in the flour and cook for a couple of minutes, then gradually stir in the stock. Bring to a boil and simmer for at least 30 minutes, until the broth is deeply flavored. Season to taste with salt and pepper and stir in the brandy, if using.

2 Pour the soup into 4 soup bowls and place the bread croutons on top, then sprinkle generously with the cheese. Place under the broiler until browned and bubbling. Serve straight away.

CORN AND SMOKED HADDOCK SOUP

This is a wonderfully comforting soup.

Serves 4

4 corn cobs (or about 14 ounces frozen corn)

11 ounces smoked haddock

3⅓ cups milk

2 tablespoons unsalted butter

2 shallots, finely chopped

1 teaspoon sugar

1 bay leaf

¾ cup heavy cream

8 slices of very thin pancetta, diced and fried till crisp (optional)

sea salt and black pepper

chopped parsley, to garnish

1 Take the corn kernels off the cobs – the easiest way to do this is to hold the corn upright on a board and cut down its length with a sharp knife.

2 Put the haddock in a wide pan, pour over the milk and bring to a simmer. Cover and cook very gently for 3–4 minutes, until the haddock is tender, then drain, reserving the milk. Remove the skin and any bones from the fish and flake the flesh.

3 Melt the butter in a large pan, add the shallots and cook gently until softened. Add the corn, the reserved milk, sugar and bay leaf. Bring to a boil and simmer for 10 minutes, then scoop out about a quarter of the corn with a slotted spoon and set aside. Remove the bay leaf and purée the soup in a blender. Return to a clean pan and season well. Reheat the soup, adding the cream, the reserved corn and the flaked haddock. Divide between 4 soup plates, sprinkle with the pancetta, if using, and garnish with the parsley.

PEA AND HAM SOUP

This recipe is a quick version using chicken stock, but the traditional way to do it is to boil up your own ham knucklebone and use the water for the soup.

Serves 4

4 tablespoons unsalted butter

1 onion, finely chopped

2 celery sticks, finely chopped

4 ounces cooked ham, chopped

7 ounces frozen peas, defrosted

8 mint leaves

1¾ cups chicken stock (see pages 30–31)

1½ cups milk

⅓ cup heavy cream (optional)

sea salt and white pepper

finely chopped chives, to garnish

Melt the butter in a saucepan, add the onion and celery and cook gently for about 5 minutes, until soft. Stir in the ham, peas and mint leaves, then add the chicken stock and milk. Simmer for about 15 minutes on a low heat. Allow to cool a little, then strain about half the liquid into a clean saucepan. Put the rest of the soup into a blender and purée until smooth. Add to the liquid in the saucepan and reheat gently. Stir in the cream, if using, and season to taste with salt and pepper. Serve garnished with very finely chopped chives.

CREAMED WILD MUSHROOM SOUP

Mushroom soup is considered a little old-fashioned now, but it's so soothing and packed full of flavor that it's worth rediscovering.

Serves 6

4 tablespoons unsalted butter

1 onion, finely chopped

9 ounces button mushrooms, roughly chopped

9 ounces wild mushrooms, roughly chopped

2 sprigs of thyme

2 garlic cloves, finely chopped

2 cups milk

2 cups chicken stock (see pages 30–31)

1¼ cups heavy cream

sea salt and black pepper

1 Melt the butter in a large saucepan, add the onion and cook gently until softened. Stir in the mushrooms, thyme and garlic and cook for a minute longer, then add the milk and stock and bring to a boil. Reduce the heat and simmer for 20 minutes.

2 Season well with salt and pepper and cool slightly, then purée in a blender, in batches, until smooth. Now pass the soup through a fine sieve back into the saucepan and add the cream. Reheat gently, then taste and adjust the seasoning.

WHITE SAUCES

A white, or béchamel, sauce is one of the basic recipes we all need to know. It is endlessly versatile and, because the flavor is so neutral, it makes a good base for lots of different flavors — from the classic cheese to herbs, spices, even cooked spinach. Use a white sauce in gratins, soufflés, to bind croquettes, or simply to sauce meat, fish or vegetables.

This is the classic way to make a white sauce — infusing the milk with herbs, onion and peppercorns to give a deep, aromatic flavor before combining it with a roux. The unusual crust on the fish pie provides a delicious twist on an old favorite.

FISH PIE

with walnut and parmesan crust

To make the basic Béchamel Sauce, follow steps 1 to 11

SERVES 4–6

1½ pounds white fish fillets (such as haddock, pollack, hake or sole), skinned

½ pound undyed smoked haddock fillet, skinned

3 tablespoons unsalted butter, melted

½ cup Fish Stock (see page 35)

3½ tablespoons chopped parsley

3½ tablespoons crème fraîche

5 ounces shelled cooked shrimp, preferably large ones

sea salt and black pepper

FOR THE BÉCHAMEL SAUCE:

2 cups whole milk

2 bay leaves

½ onion, peeled and cut in half

6 white peppercorns

a sprig of thyme

3 tablespoons unsalted butter

1.5 ounces all-purpose flour

sea salt and white pepper

FOR THE WALNUT AND PARMESAN CRUST:

2 tablespoons unsalted butter

1 onion, finely chopped

5 tablespoons finely chopped parsley

2 ounces walnuts, crushed

2 ounces breadcrumbs

2½ tablespoons grated Cheddar cheese

5 tablespoons grated Parmesan cheese

1 egg yolk

a pinch of cayenne pepper

1 Pour the milk into a saucepan and add the bay leaves, onion, white peppercorns and thyme.

2 Bring slowly to simmering point.

3 Remove from the heat and leave to infuse for as long as possible.

4 Strain the infused milk into a glass.

5 Gently melt the butter in a heavy-bottomed saucepan. Add the flour and cook, stirring, over a low heat for 1 minute, without browning.

6 Gradually add the infused milk, stirring constantly with a wooden spoon.

7 Make sure the mixture is smooth and well blended each time before you make the next addition.

8 When all the milk has been added, continue stirring until you have a smooth, silky cream.

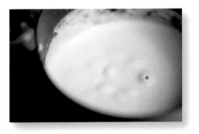

9 Bring to a boil and simmer on a low heat for 2 minutes; this helps round off the flavor.

10 Season the sauce to taste with salt and white pepper.

11 Remove from the heat.

12 Preheat the oven to 350°F. Cut the fish into large chunks. Put them into a gratin dish in a single layer.

13 Season the fish with salt and pepper, pour over the melted butter and fish stock.

14 Cover the dish with foil.

15 Place in the oven and bake for about 15 minutes, until the fish is only just cooked. Remove from the oven and leave to rest for a few minutes.

16 To make the crust, melt the butter in a frying pan.

17 Add the onion and cook gently until softened.

18 Put the fried onion into a bowl with all the remaining ingredients, mix well and season to taste with salt and pepper.

19 Pour off all the juices from the gratin dish containing the fish and set aside.

20 Gently reheat the béchamel sauce, if necessary, then add 5–7 tablespoons of the fishy juices to it – but be careful not to thin down the sauce too much.

21 Stir in the parsley and crème fraîche and season to taste.

22 Add the shrimp to the fish.

23 Pour the sauce over the top.

24 Scatter over the crust. Place in the oven and bake for about 25 minutes, until browned and bubbling.

béchamel sauce variations

Cheese Sauce (Mornay Sauce) – stir 3.5 ounces grated Gruyère or Cheddar (or a mixture of Gruyère or Cheddar and Parmesan) into the hot Béchamel Sauce until melted; do not let it boil after adding the cheese or it will become stringy. Season with 1 teaspoon Dijon mustard.

Parsley Sauce – add a few parsley stalks to the flavorings for the milk. Stir 6 heaping tablespoons finely chopped parsley into the Béchamel Sauce, together with 1 teaspoon lemon juice and 2½ tablespoons heavy cream.

Soubise Sauce – cook 11 ounces finely chopped onions in 2 tablespoons butter until very soft but not colored; this will take at least 20 minutes. Stir them into the Béchamel Sauce and cook very gently for 15 minutes, then push the mixture through a fine sieve or whiz with a hand blender. Reheat and season to taste with salt, pepper and nutmeg. You could stir in a little heavy cream, if you like.

Spinach Sauce – remove the stalks from 18 ounces fresh spinach and cook the leaves in a large pan of boiling salted water for just 1 minute, until wilted. Drain, refresh in cold water, then squeeze out all the excess liquid. Chop finely and stir into the Béchamel Sauce, together with a little heavy cream, if desired.

Mustard Sauce – add 2½ tablespoons Dijon mustard, 1 teaspoon mustard powder, 5 tablespoons heavy cream and 1 teaspoon vinegar or lemon juice to the Béchamel Sauce.

TIPS AND IDEAS

■ Traditionally the onion is studded with a few cloves before infusing the milk. This gives too strong a flavor to use in a fish pie but, if you like cloves, you can try including them for other dishes.

■ Adding the milk gradually should ensure the sauce stays lump free. But if you do end up with lumps, put the sauce through a sieve or use a hand blender to smooth it out.

■ If you are not using the sauce immediately, transfer it to a bowl and press a piece of plastic wrap on the surface to stop a skin from forming.

■ Béchamel sauce freezes well and can be defrosted quickly in the microwave. Don't keep it for more than 4 days in the fridge, however, or it will taste stale.

■ A variation on a roux is *beurre manié*, or 'kneaded butter' – equal quantities of soft butter and plain flour beaten together. Shape the mixture into a log and keep it in the fridge, wrapped in plastic wrap, for up to 3 weeks. You can slice off little pieces and whisk them into soups, sauces and stews to thicken them.

CAULIFLOWER CHEESE

This warming dish is very easy to make and, in my experience, children love it. My mother always used to serve a whole cauliflower on a plate, complete with leaves, and pour the sauce over the top. I have to say, I prefer to serve separate florets.

Serves 4

1 cauliflower

3¼ cups milk

3½ tablespoons unsalted butter

1.5 ounces all-purpose flour

5 tablespoons grated Gruyère cheese

a pinch of cayenne pepper

5 tablespoons breadcrumbs

sea salt and black pepper

1 First cut the cauliflower into florets, put them into a saucepan and cover with the milk. Simmer for 10 minutes until soft, then strain the milk into a bowl. Put the cauliflower into a gratin dish and leave on one side.

2 Now to make the béchamel: melt the butter in a small pan over a low heat, then add the flour, stirring to make a roux. Cook gently for 2 minutes, then gradually add the reserved milk from the cauliflower, stirring constantly. Bring to a boil, then reduce the heat and simmer for 5 minutes, until thickened. Season well with salt and pepper, pour the sauce over the cauliflower and sprinkle with the Gruyère cheese, cayenne and breadcrumbs. Place in an oven preheated to 350°F and bake for 20–25 minutes, until the top is golden.

MACARONI AND CHEESE WITH BACON

This is the ultimate cupboard dish. It's lovely with smoked bacon but you can use whatever you have available – anchovies, different cheeses, roasted peppers and spinach are all good. Or simply add lots of fresh herbs to the sauce.

Serves 4

6 slices of smoked bacon

olive oil

9 ounces macaroni

1 quantity of Béchamel Sauce (see pages 44–45), made with 3½ tablespoons butter, 1.5 ounces all-purpose flour and 2⅔ cups milk

8 ounces Cheddar cheese, grated

5 tablespoons freshly grated Parmesan cheese

1 teaspoon grated nutmeg

a pinch of cayenne pepper

butter for greasing

1 First cut the bacon in small pieces and fry in a little olive oil in a non-stick frying pan until crisp. Remove and put to one side.

2 Cook the macaroni in a large pan of boiling salted water according to the instructions on page 135. Meanwhile, reheat the béchamel sauce if necessary, then stir in 5 ounces of the Cheddar cheese plus the Parmesan, nutmeg and cayenne.

3 Drain the pasta, return it to the pan and mix in the cheese sauce and bacon. Season well with salt and pepper, then transfer the mixture to a buttered gratin dish and sprinkle on the rest of the Cheddar. Bake in an oven preheated to 400°F for 20 minutes or until golden brown.

MOUSSAKA

I find this dish easier to assemble if the meat is cold, so you can cook it well in advance, if you like.

Serves 4

2¼ pounds eggplant, cut into slices ¼ inch thick

olive oil for frying

2 onions, finely chopped

1½ pounds ground lamb

4 garlic cloves, finely chopped

1 tablespoon crushed coriander

2½ tablespoons chopped oregano

14-ounce can of chopped tomatoes

3½ tablespoons tomato paste

sea salt and black pepper

For the sauce:

½ quantity of Béchamel Sauce (see pages 44–45)

3.5 ounces feta cheese

½ teaspoon freshly grated nutmeg

1 First cook the eggplant slices. You can either brush them with oil and bake them for 20–25 minutes in an oven preheated to 350°F, turning them over halfway through, or you can fry them in hot oil. This will take less time but it will use up more oil. The eggplant should be golden brown and tender.

2 Heat a couple of tablespoons of olive oil in a large saucepan, add the onions and cook gently until softened. Add the minced lamb, raise the heat and separate the strands of meat with a fork. Don't crowd the pan; fry the lamb in 2 batches if necessary.

3 Add the garlic, coriander, oregano and tomatoes. Mix well and bring to a simmer. Cover and cook for about 40 minutes, stirring occasionally and removing the lid after 15 minutes. Mix in the tomato paste, season well with salt and pepper and cook for a further 10 minutes, stirring all the time. Remove from the heat and leave to cool.

4 To make the sauce, gently reheat the béchamel, if necessary. Crumble in the feta cheese, add the nutmeg and season to taste with salt and pepper – remember, the cheese is quite salty.

5 To assemble the moussaka, put a layer of eggplant slices in an ovenproof dish about 8 inches x 10 inches, and top with half the lamb. Add another layer of eggplant, then the remaining lamb and finish with a layer of eggplant. Pour on the sauce.

6 Bake in an oven preheated to 350°F for about 40 minutes, until browned and bubbling. Serve with a green salad (see pages 12–13).

GUINEA FOWL AND FENNEL FRICASSEE

Serves 4

2½ tablespoons olive oil

6 tablespoons unsalted butter

1 guinea fowl, cut into 8 pieces

2 fennel bulbs, finely sliced lengthwise

1 onion, sliced

8 green onions, finely chopped

⅔ cup white wine

about 3⅓ cups chicken stock (see pages 30–31)

1 ounce all-purpose flour

sea salt and black pepper

2½ tablespoons finely chopped chives, to garnish

1 Heat the olive oil and 2 tablespoons of the butter in a large, heavy-bottomed saucepan, add the guinea fowl pieces and brown them on all sides (do this in batches, if necessary). Remove and set aside. Melt 2 tablespoons of the remaining butter in the pan, add the fennel and cook gently until softened but not browned. Remove and set aside with the guinea fowl. Cook the onion in the saucepan until softened, then put the fennel and guinea fowl back in and add the green onions. Pour in the white wine, bring to a simmer and cook for 3 minutes. Pour in enough chicken stock just to cover, bring to a boil, then reduce the heat and cook gently for 20 minutes or until the guinea fowl is cooked through.

2 Strain the stock from the pan into a glass, leaving the guinea fowl and vegetables behind. Season the stock with salt and pepper. Melt the remaining 2 tablespoons butter in a medium saucepan, add the flour and cook, stirring, over a low heat for 1 minute to make a roux. Gradually stir in about 1 2/3 cups of the strained stock until you have a thick sauce. Bring to a boil and simmer for a few minutes, then season well. Pour the sauce over the guinea fowl and fennel and heat thoroughly for 5 minutes. To serve, transfer to a gratin dish, if you like, and sprinkle with the chopped chives.

TURKEY CROQUETTES

Depending on the dryness of your meat, you might need to add a little more béchamel here. Add it gradually, until the mixture holds together, but be careful not to overdo it.

Serves 4

14 ounces cooked turkey

3.5 ounces cooked ham

1 tablespoon softened unsalted butter

about 5 ounces leftover Béchamel Sauce (see pages 44–45)

1 tablespoon chopped parsley

3 eggs

3.5 ounces all-purpose flour

7 ounces white breadcrumbs

sunflower oil for deep-frying

sea salt and black pepper

1 Chop the turkey and ham very finely by hand or put them into a food processor and pulse until finely chopped but not a mush. Transfer to a bowl and mix in the butter, 5 ounces of béchamel and the parsley. If the mixture doesn't hold together, add a little more sauce. Season well with salt and pepper, then chill for about 2 hours, until firm.

2 Remove the mixture from the fridge and shape it into croquettes about 2 1/2 inches long and 1 inch wide. Put them back into the fridge again to chill.

3 Whisk the eggs in a bowl, put the flour on a plate and put the breadcrumbs into a large shallow dish. To coat the croquettes, roll them in the flour, then in the egg, letting the excess run off, then finally in the breadcrumbs. Repeat the whole process once – this will give an extra-crisp coating.

4 Heat some oil to 340°F in a deep-fat fryer or a large deep saucepan – if using a saucepan, don't fill it more than about a third full. Fry the croquettes in batches until golden brown, then remove and drain on kitchen paper.

5 The croquettes can be cooked in advance and then reheated in a moderate oven.

EMULSION SAUCES

Warm emulsion sauces such as hollandaise and
sabayon rely on gradually whisking melted butter
or alcohol into egg yolks to create a silky, creamy
sauce. You can add numerous flavorings — from
the classic tarragon of a Béarnaise sauce to
ginger, orange or whatever takes your fancy.
Emulsion sauces can make people nervous,
and it's true they can be tricky, because if you
overheat the egg yolks they can split. Follow the
step-by-step instructions in this chapter and you
should be fine.

This recipe showcases both the hollandaise sauce and good, very fresh asparagus — they make perfect companions for each other. Asparagus has an extremely short season, from late spring to mid summer, so do take advantage of it.

Asparagus with
HOLLANDAISE SAUCE

To make the basic Hollandaise Sauce, follow steps 2 to 17

SERVES 4

28 asparagus spears

FOR THE HOLLANDAISE SAUCE:

9 ounces unsalted butter

2½ tablespoons white wine vinegar

2½ tablespoons water

1 bay leaf

1 teaspoon white peppercorns

4 medium egg yolks

juice of 1 lemon, or to taste

sea salt and white pepper

 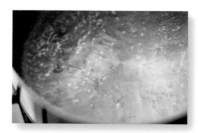 

1 Trim the asparagus by breaking off the lower woody part of each stem.

2 Put a large pan of salted water on to boil so you can cook the asparagus as soon as the sauce is made.

3 For the hollandaise sauce, first clarify the butter. Put the butter in a small, heavy-bottomed pan over a very low heat.

4 Leave until it has completely melted and the milky residue has separated.

5 Skim off any froth from the top and pour off the clear butter, leaving the residue behind (this can be discarded).

6 Let the clarified butter cool slightly.

7 Put the vinegar, water, bay leaf and white peppercorns into a small, heavy-bottomed pan.

8 Bring to a boil.

9 When the liquid has reduced to a tablespoon, strain it into a bowl and allow to cool slightly.

10 Set a medium-sized bowl over a pan of simmering water, making sure the water doesn't touch the base of the bowl.

11 Pour the reduction into the bowl and switch off the heat (the gentle heat from the hot water beneath the bowl will be enough to cook the hollandaise).

12 Lightly whisk the egg yolks.

13 Add them to the reduction.

14 Stir until they start to thicken slightly to a cream.

15 Very slowly pour in the clarified butter, whisking constantly with a balloon whisk.

16 If the mixture is becoming too thick, briefly turn the heat back on low but make sure the hollandaise doesn't overheat – you do not want the sauce to separate after all your hard work (if it does separate, it can be rescued – see Tips and Ideas below).

17 When all the butter has been added, stir in the lemon juice and season well with salt and white pepper.

18 Add the asparagus to the pan of boiling water and cook for 1–2 minutes. It should be quite *al dente*. Drain well and serve immediately, with the hollandaise.

TIPS AND IDEAS

■ Don't be tempted to skip the vinegar reduction; it helps bind the egg yolks together and adds flavor.

■ When mixing the egg yolks into the reduction, don't overheat or they will become scrambled; they should thicken only very slightly.

■ Adding the butter really slowly should prevent the sauce from curdling. If it does look as if it's beginning to curdle, whisk vigorously to bring it back together. If all else fails, start again with another egg yolk in the bowl and gradually whisk the curdled mixture into it.

■ Once you feel confident preparing hollandaise sauce and judging the correct heat level, you could make it directly in a saucepan. It's vital to use a good-quality, heavy-bottomed pan, though, and to take it off the heat once you have mixed the egg yolks into the reduction. If the sauce becomes too thick while you are adding the butter, simply return it to a very low heat for a few seconds.

■ You can make a quick hollandaise sauce in a food processor, though it won't be as thick: put the strained reduction and the egg yolks in the food processor and whiz briefly to combine. Bring the butter to a boil in a pan (there is no need to clarify it in this instance) and pour it slowly on to the egg yolks with the processor running. Season well with salt, pepper and lemon juice.

■ Add any flavorings right at the end (see page 60).

■ Hollandaise is delicious served with eggs, fish, lobster, lamb, or vegetables such as braised fennel or carrots with dill.

■ Hollandaise does not keep but you can 'hold' it for up to an hour – either leave it in its bowl over the pan of hot water, store it in a Thermos bottle, or stir in a little cream or béchamel sauce (see pages 44–45) to stabilize it.

hollandaise sauce variations

Béarnaise Sauce – add 1 finely chopped shallot and 2½ tablespoons chopped tarragon to the reduction, then stir 2½ more tablespoons chopped tarragon into the finished sauce.

Mild Mustard Sauce – stir 2½ tablespoons Dijon mustard into the Hollandaise Sauce. Delicious with chicken or pork.

Mousseline Sauce – fold 3½ tablespoons whipped heavy cream into the Hollandaise Sauce just before serving. This is very good with all fish.

Ginger Hollandaise Sauce – stir 1 tablespoon ginger syrup into the Hollandaise Sauce. Serve with white fish.

Maltaise Sauce – stir the juice of ½ orange, the grated zest of 1 orange and 1 teaspoon Cointreau into the Hollandaise Sauce. Serve with oily fish.

JUST-COOKED BOILED EGGS WITH HOLLANDAISE AND PARSLEY

This is the simplest starter of all but if it is done perfectly it is delicious.

Serves 4

6 medium eggs

1 quantity of Hollandaise Sauce (see pages 56–58)

2½ tablespoons small capers, rinsed and drained

4 handfuls of mâche (lamb's lettuce)

2½ tablespoons finely chopped parsley

1 Boil the eggs for 8 minutes; this should give yolks that are still slightly soft. Drain and put into ice water to cool down quickly. Make up the hollandaise and stir in the capers. Shell the eggs and cut them lengthwise in half.

2 Put a handful of mâche on each serving plate with 3 egg halves in the middle. Pour over the hollandaise and sprinkle with parsley.

SEARED GRAY MULLET WITH CAVOLO NERO AND GINGER HOLLANDAISE

This is a quick but very impressive dish. Mullet works well but you can also use firm white fish such as sea bass.

Serves 4

4 gray (or red) mullet, weighing about 14 ounces each, scaled and filleted (ask your fishmonger to do this)

all-purpose flour, for dusting

2½ tablespoons olive oil

14 ounces cavolo nero (kale)

1 quantity of Ginger Hollandaise Sauce (see pages 60)

4 tablespoons unsalted butter

sea salt and black pepper

1 Score the fish fillets by slashing the skin of each one 2 or 3 times with a very sharp knife, being careful not to cut through the flesh. Season with salt and pepper. Dust the skin side only with flour. Heat the olive oil in a large frying pan, lay the fish in it, skin-side down, and cook over a medium heat for about 2 minutes, until golden brown. Turn over and cook for 30 seconds longer, then place on a baking tray and set aside.

2 To cook the cavolo nero, tear the leaves off the stalks, then add them to a large pan of boiling salted water and cook for 4 minutes. Drain well.

3 Prepare the hollandaise as described on pages 56–59 and 60. When it is ready, put the mullet into an oven preheated to 375°F for 2 minutes to heat through. Melt the butter in a saucepan, add the cavolo nero, season well with salt and pepper and heat thoroughly. Divide the cavolo nero between 4 plates, top with the mullet and serve with the ginger hollandaise.

EGGS BENEDICT

Although this is a simple dish to make, there are quite a lot of last-minute details to attend to. You can make things easier for yourself by poaching the eggs well in advance and reheating them (see page 66) and cooking the Canadian bacon first, then keeping it warm in the oven. That means you can concentrate on making the hollandaise sauce, then simply toast the muffins when you're ready to serve.

Serves 4

8 slices of smoky Canadian bacon or slices of ham

a little olive oil, if needed

4 eggs

4 English muffins, split in half

1 quantity of Hollandaise Sauce (see pages 56–58)

finely chopped parsley, to garnish

1 If using Canadian bacon, fry it in a little olive oil until crisp. Remove and keep warm. Now poach the eggs according to the instructions on page 66.

2 Toast the muffins, put them on to 4 warmed serving plates and top each half with a slice of Canadian bacon or ham. Top with the poached eggs and spoon over the hollandaise. Sprinkle with chopped parsley and serve.

ICED ZABAGLIONE

I absolutely love this. The wonderful thing about it is that you can get it ready in advance and keep it in the glasses in the freezer. What you don't want is to have it frozen solid, so don't put it in too far in advance. The zabaglione mixture should be light and airy, so make sure you whisk until it has completely cooled down.

Serves 4–6

4 egg yolks

3.5 ounces superfine sugar

⅔ cup dry Marsala

⅔ cup whipping cream

1 Put the egg yolks and sugar in a large glass or stainless steel bowl and whisk, preferably with an electric beater, until pale and thick. Add the Marsala and then place the bowl over a pan of simmering water, making sure the water doesn't touch the base of the bowl. Whisk constantly until the mixture has doubled in volume. Remove from the heat and continue whisking until cool.

2 In a separate bowl, whip the cream until it is thick enough to hold its shape, then fold it into the zabaglione. Pour into glasses, filling them to about 1/2 inch from the top, and freeze for 1 1/2–2 hours, until ice cold but not frozen solid.

SUMMER BERRIES WITH GRAND MARNIER SABAYON

Other fruits work well here too. Oranges and figs are particularly good.

Serves 4

5 tablespoons balsamic vinegar

7 ounces strawberries

7 ounces raspberries

7 ounces redcurrants or cranberries

1 tablespoon superfine sugar

For the sabayon:

4 egg yolks

1.5 ounces superfine sugar

½ cup Grand Marnier

1 Put the balsamic vinegar in a small pan and simmer until reduced to about 2 teaspoons. Don't worry about the smell! – it will smell very potent but the vinegar will sweeten and become mellower as it reduces and thickens. Put all the fruit in a bowl, add the vinegar and sugar and toss gently. Set aside.

2 Put all the ingredients for the sabayon in a large glass or stainless steel bowl, then rest it over a pan of gently simmering water, making sure the water isn't touching the base of the bowl. Whisk continuously with a balloon whisk or a handheld electric beater until the sabayon is pale and creamy; it should be thick enough to cling to the whisk when it is raised from the bowl. Remove from the heat and continue to whisk until the sabayon has cooled to room temperature; this helps to stabilize the mixture.

3 Spread the berries on to 4 large plates. Pour the sabayon over the top, then caramelize lightly with a kitchen blowtorch or under a hot grill. Serve immediately.

EGGS

Egg dishes are some of the easiest to make but also the easiest to get wrong. So this chapter goes back to basics, with step-by-step instructions on making perfect poached eggs, proper scrambled eggs — creamy and soft, not hard and rubbery — and light and fluffy French omelettes. With the techniques at your fingertips and a box of good, fresh eggs, you will never be short of an almost-instant meal again.

It's vital to use fresh eggs for poaching – the freshest eggs will give the loveliest plump, round shape. People often ask me how to poach eggs. Here's how!

POACHED EGGS

1 Fill a medium saucepan three-quarters full with water. Add 2½ teaspoons of white wine vinegar. Bring to the boil, then turn the heat down to a simmer.

2 Crack an egg into a small bowl.

3 Draw a long-handled spoon through the water in a circular motion to create a vortex.

TIPS AND IDEAS

■ You can poach eggs in advance if you transfer them to a bowl of ice water as soon as they are cooked. They will keep in the fridge for 2 days, as long as you change the water every day. To reheat, put into simmering water for 40 seconds.

4 Tip the egg into the water.

5 Continue stirring round the egg once or twice so the white attaches itself to the yolk. The egg will take up to 2½ minutes to cook.

■ Store eggs in a cool place, but preferably not the fridge. If you do keep them in the fridge, bring them back to room temperature before cooking.

■ Most eggs you buy are stamped with a 'best-before' date, which is usually 4 weeks after they are laid. To check an egg for freshness, put it in a bowl of cold water; if it floats, it is stale. This doesn't mean it can't be used – but that it's not ideal for poaching (if an egg is actually off, the smell will be unmistakable).

6 To check it's done, lift the egg out with a slotted spoon. Gently press the white to make sure it's cooked through.

7 Rest the spoon on a folded tea towel for a minute, so all the water is absorbed, then serve.

The trick to making good scrambled eggs is to cook them slowly and gently in a non-stick pan, as this is what makes them creamy. Cooked this way, they are a real feast.

≈ SCRAMBLED EGGS ≈

SERVES 2

3 tablespoons unsalted butter

5 large eggs

sea salt and pepper

buttered toast, to serve

a little chopped parsley, to garnish (optional)

1 Melt the butter in a small, non-stick frying pan over a low heat.

2 Break the eggs into a bowl and add a pinch of salt and pepper.

3 Whisk together with a balloon whisk or fork.

4 Pour the eggs into the pan and leave undisturbed for 10 seconds.

5 Start to go backwards and forwards with a wooden spoon, keeping the heat very low and making sure the spoon gets right into the edges of the pan.

6 When the eggs become very creamy but are still quite runny, remove the pan from the heat and keep stirring for a minute or so.

Omelettes take just five minutes to prepare and are a perfect swift supper. Choose from the fillings on page 72, or add whatever you fancy.

⤙ FRENCH OMELETTE ⤚

SERVES 1

3 large eggs

1 tablespoon unsalted butter

filling of your choice (see page 72)

sea salt and pepper

1 Break the eggs into a bowl.

2 Whisk them together with a fork or a balloon whisk and season with salt and pepper.

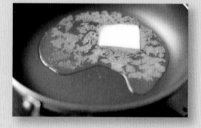

3 Melt the butter in a 7–8-inch non-stick frying pan over a low heat.

4 Pour in the eggs, let them sit for 10 seconds, then start to draw in the set egg from the sides of the pan with a fork so the uncooked egg from the center runs out to the sides.

5 When the omelette is pale golden underneath and set but still slightly undercooked and creamy in the center, add your filling.

6 Then fold the omelette in half and leave for 30 seconds or so. Turn the omelette out on to a plate and eat immediately.

french omelette fillings

Cheese Omelette – add 1 ounce grated Cheddar or Gruyère or crumbled goat cheese to the omelette before folding.

Herb Omelette – add a handful of finely chopped herbs (chives, parsley, tarragon or whatever you like) to the raw eggs.

Shrimp Omelette – heat 1 tablespoon butter in a small pan, then toss in 2 ounces cooked shrimp and some chopped parsley and heat through. Add to the omelette before folding.

Mushroom Omelette – heat 1 tablespoon butter in a non-stick pan, add 2 ounces sliced mushrooms – any type, depending on what is in season – and some salt and pepper. Cook over medium heat for 3 minutes or until tender. Drain if necessary and add to the omelette before folding.

BOILED EGGS

Make sure your eggs are at room temperature. Using a large spoon, carefully add them to a pan of gently simmering water. For soft-boiled eggs, allow 4 1/2 minutes for medium eggs and 5 minutes for large. Hard-boiled eggs take around 10 minutes.

TIPS AND IDEAS

■ To make sure the eggs don't crack when they meet the boiling water, have them at room temperature and keep the water at a gentle simmer. If the egg does crack, add a good pinch of salt to the water to help prevent the white from running out.

■ When you drain hard-boiled eggs, run them under cold water straight away to prevent a gray ring from forming around the yolk.

■ Quail's eggs should be boiled for 2 minutes if you want them soft-boiled and 3 minutes for hard.

■ When I was young, I was always told to bash my boiled egg with a spoon immediately to stop it cooking further.

TORTILLA WITH CHORIZO

This is a great supper dish. Chorizo and eggs are a match made in heaven.

Serves 4

5 tablespoons olive oil

18 ounces waxy potatoes, peeled and cut into ¾-inch dice

5 ounces onions, sliced

2 garlic cloves, crushed

11 ounces chorizo, sliced

7 medium eggs

2½ tablespoons finely chopped flat-leaf parsley

sea salt and black pepper

1 Preheat the oven to 325°F. Heat 3 tablespoons of the olive oil in a large, heavy-bottomed, ovenproof frying pan, add the potatoes and cook gently, without browning, until tender. This can take up to 20 minutes. Once the potatoes are done, transfer them to a plate.

2 Heat another tablespoon of the oil in the pan, add the onions and garlic and cook gently for about 5 minutes, until softened. Now stir in the chorizo and fry until the oil runs out. Add the onion and chorizo to the potatoes.

3 Lightly whisk the eggs together and season well with salt and pepper. Stir in the potatoes, onions, chorizo and parsley. Wipe the frying pan clean, add the remaining tablespoon of olive oil and place over a low heat. Pour the omelette mixture into the pan and cook on a low heat for about 5 minutes, until it is set underneath. Transfer the pan to the oven and cook for 5 minutes, until almost set on top. Remove, invert the omelette onto a plate – carefully loosen the edges first with a spatula if necessary – then slide it back into the pan. Place over a low heat for 3 minutes or until set, then serve. It's good warm or at room temperature.

SOFT QUAIL'S EGGS WITH CELERY SALT

Serves 4

12 quail's eggs

2 Little Gem lettuces, shredded

celery salt

1 quantity of Mayonnaise (see pages 16–17) – optional

1 Add the eggs to a pan of boiling water and simmer for 2 minutes, then drain and put into ice water. To remove the shells, take them off as a spiral, going round and round – be gentle and you are less likely to damage the eggs.

2 Divide the shredded lettuce between 4 plates, top with the eggs, then sprinkle with celery salt and serve – with some mayonnaise on the side, if you like.

tortilla variations

Tortilla with Red Peppers and Black Olives – follow the recipe to the left, omitting the chorizo and adding 2 sliced red peppers to the onion once softened. Cook until they are tender, then add to the potatoes along with 12 chopped black olives and 3½ tablespoons chopped flat-leaf parsley.

Tortilla with Artichokes and Cilantro – follow the recipe to the left, omitting the chorizo and stirring 8 cooked artichoke hearts (canned ones are fine) and 2½ tablespoons chopped cilantro into the potato mixture.

SCOTCH EGGS

Home-made scotch eggs are just the best.

Makes 8

8 medium eggs

2 tablespoons unsalted butter

1 onion, finely chopped

16 ounces sausage meat

2½ tablespoons finely chopped parsley

1 tablespoon finely chopped thyme

sunflower oil for deep-frying

sea salt and black pepper

For the coating:

4 eggs

9 ounces breadcrumbs

1 Boil the medium eggs for 8 minutes as described on page 72, then drain and refresh in cold water. Remove the shells and set aside.

2 Melt the butter in a frying pan, add the onion and cook gently until softened but not browned. Remove from the heat.

3 Put the sausage meat, fried onion and herbs in a bowl, add plenty of seasoning and mix well. Divide the mixture into 8 pieces. Flatten out each one and roll it around an egg, bringing it together so there are no gaps. If you dampen your hands slightly and go around again, it gives a smoother finish. Put the coated eggs on to a tray and chill for a couple of hours.

4 For the final coating, whisk the eggs in a bowl and season well; put the breadcrumbs into a large dish. Roll each scotch egg in the beaten egg, drain off any excess, then put it in the breadcrumbs and turn to coat well. Repeat the process to give them a thicker coating, then chill for 30 minutes.

5 Heat some sunflower oil in a deep-fat fryer or a large, deep saucepan to 325–350°F – no higher, otherwise the exterior will brown before the sausage meat is cooked through. Fry the eggs, in batches, for about 5 minutes, then drain on kitchen paper and leave to cool.

GREEN BEAN, PINE NUT AND POACHED EGG SALAD

A great little supper dish or starter.

Serves 2

7 ounces fine green beans, trimmed

1 garlic clove, very finely chopped

1 tablespoon extra virgin olive oil

1.5 ounces pine nuts

2 slices of Serrano ham, cut into quarters

a good handful of arugula

2 eggs

1 ounce Parmesan cheese, cut into shavings with a vegetable peeler

fine sea salt and black pepper

For the dressing:

3½ tablespoons extra virgin olive oil

½ tablespoon balsamic vinegar

1 Cook the beans in a pan of boiling water for about 3 minutes, until tender (I prefer them not to be *al dente* for this salad). Drain them very well and, while they are still warm, add the garlic, a pinch of salt, 1 teaspoon of ground black pepper and the extra virgin olive oil. Mix well and set aside to cool.

2 Whisk the ingredients for the dressing together and season to taste with salt and pepper. Lightly toast the pine nuts in a small dry frying pan until golden. Toss half of them with the green beans, retaining the other half for garnish. Toss the Serrano ham with the beans, being careful not to mix too much, so it doesn't flatten. Finally toss in the arugula.

3 Poach the eggs according to the instructions on page 66. Divide the salad between 2 plates, top with the poached eggs and surround with the dressing. Garnish with the Parmesan shavings and the remaining pine nuts.

ZUCCHINI, FENNEL AND TARRAGON FRITTATA

A frittata is the Italian equivalent of the Spanish tortilla. You can add whatever filling you like but be careful not to overload it with too many flavors at once.

Serves 4

3½ tablespoons olive oil

1 onion, sliced

1 fennel bulb, finely sliced

18 ounces zucchini, roughly diced

6 eggs

a handful of tarragon, finely chopped

sea salt and black pepper

1 Heat 2 tablespoons of the olive oil in a frying pan about 8 inches in diameter, add the onion and fennel and cook until soft but not browned. This will take at least 20 minutes. Add the zucchini to the pan, along with the final tablespoon of oil, and cook for 5 minutes, until it just begins to soften.

2 Whisk the eggs together in a bowl and season well with salt and pepper. Add the tarragon, then pour this mixture into the frying pan. Gently move everything around a little, then leave to cook on a low heat for 6–8 minutes, until the egg is almost set but still very soft on top. Invert the frittata onto a plate and then slide it back into the pan. Continue to cook for another 3 minutes or so, until set, then turn out on to a plate. Serve warm or at room temperature.

---

frittata variation

Red Pepper, Onion and Spinach Frittata – follow the recipe above, omitting the fennel, zucchini and tarragon and adding 4 roasted red peppers, finely sliced, to the softened onion, followed by 2 handfuls of baby spinach.

SMOKED HADDOCK WITH POACHED EGGS

One of the great combinations. I always have this for my breakfast when I go away.

Serves 4

4 x 6.5-ounce pieces of undyed smoked haddock fillet

about 2 cups whole milk, enough to cover the fish

3 tablespoons unsalted butter

4 eggs

1 quantity of Hollandaise Sauce (see pages 56–58) – optional

4 sprigs of flat-leaf parsley, to garnish

1 Put the fish into a frying pan, add enough milk just to cover and then dot with the butter. Bring to a simmer and cook very gently for about 3 minutes, turning the fish over if necessary. Remove from the heat and leave to stand for 3 minutes to complete the cooking. Drain well.

2 Poach the eggs (see page 66) and make the hollandaise, if using. Place the haddock on 4 plates, top with the poached eggs, then spoon some hollandaise on top, if you like. Garnish with the parsley and serve.

PIPÉRADE WITH SMOKED BACON

This is a classic Spanish dish, and very tasty.

Serves 4

2 red peppers

2 green peppers

5 tablespoons olive oil

1 onion, finely sliced

2 garlic cloves, finely chopped

6 large, vine-ripened tomatoes, skinned (see page 135), deseeded and roughly chopped

1 tablespoon thyme leaves

a pinch of cayenne pepper

6 eggs

8 smoked Canadian bacon slices, fried until crisp

sea salt and black pepper

chopped parsley, to garnish

1 Put the peppers on a baking tray and place in an oven preheated to 375°F. Cook for 20 minutes, turning halfway through, until charred and blistered. Meanwhile, heat the olive oil in a heavy-bottomed casserole, add the onion and garlic and cook gently until softened.

2 Remove the skin and seeds from the peppers and roughly chop the flesh. Add to the onion, then stir in the tomatoes and cook until all their liquid has evaporated. Stir in the thyme and cayenne and season well with salt and pepper.

3 Whisk the eggs together in a bowl, season with salt and pepper and add to the vegetables. Stir gently over a low heat for 2–3 minutes, until the eggs are just beginning to set. Remove from the heat and leave to stand for a minute, then adjust the seasoning and serve immediately, garnished with the parsley and accompanied by the Canadian bacon.

SPINACH, BACON AND MUSHROOM SALAD WITH HARD-BOILED EGGS AND ANCHOVIES

Serves 4

6 bacon slices

16 ounces fresh young spinach leaves

a handful of flat-leaf parsley leaves

a handful of watercress

3.5 ounces button mushrooms, finely sliced

5–7 tablespoons Classic Vinaigrette (see pages 12–13)

4 eggs, hard-boiled (see page 72)

8 anchovies in olive oil

1 Cut the bacon into small pieces and fry until crisp, then remove from the heat.

2 Put the spinach, parsley, watercress and mushrooms into a bowl and add the bacon. Toss carefully with 4 tablespoons of vinaigrette. Cut the eggs into quarters and carefully toss into the salad. Add the anchovies and lightly toss again. Divide between 4 serving plates, drizzle with a little more vinaigrette and serve.

PANCAKES
and other
BATTERS

I was brought up eating wonderful Yorkshire pudding and pancakes, so batter played a very important part in my life. It's so versatile, and I never cease to be amazed that using just eggs, milk and flour, you end up with so many beautiful dishes. Don't save pancakes for special occasions — enjoy them as often as you can. If you have children, they will thank you for it.

To cook these pancakes, use a pancake pan or a good-quality, heavy-bottomed non-stick frying pan, 8–9 inches in diameter.

PANCAKES

stuffed with ratatouille

To make the basic Pancake Batter, follow steps 1 to 5
To cook the Pancake Batter, follow steps 6 to 10

SERVES 4

1 eggplant, cut into ½-inch dice

about ⅔ cup olive oil

2 onions, finely chopped

2 garlic cloves, finely chopped

1 red pepper, cut into ½-inch dice

1 yellow pepper, cut into ½-inch dice

2 large or 4 small zucchini, cut into ½-inch dice

8 large, vine-ripened tomatoes, skinned, deseeded and roughly chopped (see page 135)

4 sprigs of thyme

1 tablespoon tomato paste

2½ teaspoons sugar

5 tablespoons chopped basil

5 tablespoons unsalted butter, melted

9 ounces Gruyère cheese, grated

sea salt and black pepper

FOR PANCAKE BATTER (MAKES 8–10):

3.5 ounces all-purpose flour

2 medium eggs

1¼ cups whole milk

2 tablespoons unsalted butter, melted

a pinch of salt

1 teaspoon sugar

sunflower oil for frying

1 Sift the flour into a bowl.

2 Make a well in the center.

3 Whisk in the eggs one at a time with a balloon whisk to give a thick, smooth paste.

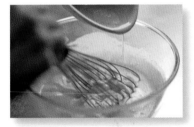

4 Now gradually whisk in the milk, followed by the melted butter.

5 Mix in the salt and sugar and then leave the batter to rest for 20 minutes.

6 Place a frying pan over a moderate heat. Put a little sunflower oil in a bowl and dip a wad of paper towel in it, then use it to grease the hot pan.

7 Pour a small ladleful of batter into the middle of the pan, tilting it quickly so the batter covers the base. Use only enough batter to cover the base thinly.

8 Turn the heat down a little and cook for a minute or so, until the pancake looks slightly set, the edges are a little frilly and the underside is pale golden.

9 Flip the pancake over with a spatula. The second side doesn't take quite so long to cook; again it should be pale golden. Turn out of the pan.

10 Stack the pancakes up, interleaved with wax paper. Repeat with the remaining batter, oiling the pan between pancakes as necessary.

11 Put the diced eggplant in a colander, sprinkle lightly with salt and leave for at least 30 minutes to draw out the water.

12 Meanwhile, drizzle some of the oil in a large, non-stick frying pan, add the onions, garlic and peppers and fry gently until soft.

13 Transfer the vegetables to a heavy-bottomed saucepan.

14 Drizzle some more oil into the pan, add the zucchini and cook until softened and slightly coloured.

15 Add to the onions and peppers, along with the tomatoes and thyme.

16 Now add the remaining oil to the frying pan and place over a fairly high heat. Pat the eggplant dry on paper towels.

17 Add it to the pan and fry until tender and golden. At first the eggplant will suck up all the oil, but eventually it will start to release the oil.

18 Add to the other vegetables and season lightly. Put the pan over a low heat and cook, uncovered, until the tomatoes have released their juices.

19 Stir in the tomato paste, sugar and basil and cook for 5 minutes longer, then taste and adjust the seasoning if necessary.

20 Leave to cool – spreading the mixture out on a baking tray will help it cool quickly.

21 Lay each pancake flat on a work surface, put a couple of tablespoons of the ratatouille on it, at the end nearest you.

22 Then fold in the sides and roll the pancake up, like a spring roll.

23 Brush a gratin dish with a little of the melted butter and lay the pancakes neatly in it. Brush the tops with the remaining melted butter.

24 Sprinkle with the Gruyère. Bake in an oven preheated to 350°F for 25–30 minutes, until the pancakes are heated through.

PANCAKES WITH ICE CREAM AND CHOCOLATE SAUCE

This is a terrific cupboard recipe.

Serves 4

1 quantity of Pancake Batter (see pages 80–81)

14 ounces vanilla ice cream

For the chocolate sauce:

3.5 ounces good-quality dark chocolate

½ cup water

6 tablespoons unsalted butter, diced

2 ounces superfine sugar

1 First make the chocolate sauce. Break up the chocolate, put it in a small pan with the water and heat gently, stirring, until melted. Add the butter and sugar and keep stirring until the butter has melted, then remove from the heat and leave to cool.

2 Cook the pancakes as described on page 81. Put a pancake on a work surface and put a spoonful of ice cream on one quarter of it. Fold the pancake over to make a half-circle and then fold the empty half underneath to form a fan shape. Using a spatula, transfer to a plate, then repeat with another pancake. Pour over some chocolate sauce and serve. Prepare the remaining pancakes in the same way.

ELDERFLOWER FRITTERS

I have an elderflower tree in my garden and it's very exciting when it comes into bloom. You can find elderflowers growing anywhere, in towns as well as in the country, but make sure you don't pick from a tree near a busy road as they will be polluted.

Serves 6–8

about 2 dozen freshly picked small elderflower heads

5 ounces self-rising flour

a pinch of salt

2.5 ounces cornstarch

1¼ cups soda water

1 egg, separated

sunflower oil for deep-frying

superfine sugar for dusting

1 Inspect the elderflower heads for insects and shake them gently to remove any dust, but don't wash them.

2 To make the batter, sift the flour, salt and cornstarch into a bowl and then gradually whisk in the soda water and egg yolk until smooth. Pour the batter through a fine sieve. Whisk the egg white to stiff peaks in a separate bowl and fold it into the batter.

3 Heat some sunflower oil to 350°F in a deep-fat fryer or a large, deep saucepan. Dip the elderflower heads in the batter, a few at a time, shake off the excess and fry in the oil until golden. Drain on paper towel, then quickly roll in superfine sugar and serve straight away.

CHERRY CLAFOUTIS

If you can buy black cherries in kirsch, they are even better in this recipe. Any fruit will do, so there are lots of alternatives: peaches, apricots, plums, and even raspberries all work well.

Serves 6

2 ounces all-purpose flour

4 eggs

⅔ cup whole milk

3.5 ounces superfine sugar

⅔ cup heavy cream

2 tablespoons softened unsalted butter

12 ounces black morello cherries from a jar, well drained

1 Sift the flour into a large bowl, then whisk in the eggs one at a time. Gradually whisk in the milk until you have a smooth batter. Mix in the superfine sugar, followed by the heavy cream.

2 Use the butter to grease a round, shallow ceramic or glass flan dish, about 8 1/2 inches in diameter. Scatter the cherries into the dish, then pour in the batter. Place in an oven preheated to 350°F and bake for 30 minutes, until the batter is golden, well risen and just set. Serve warm or at room temperature.

DROP SCONES

These are my grandchildren's absolute favorite. You'll find you can never make enough.

9 ounces self-rising flour

1 heaping teaspoon baking powder

1.5 ounces superfine sugar

a pinch of salt

2 eggs

¾ cup milk

2 tablespoons unsalted butter, melted

1 tablespoon golden syrup

sunflower oil for frying

1 Sift the flour and baking powder into a bowl, add the sugar and salt and make a well in the center. Whisk in the eggs one at a time with a balloon whisk to give a thick, smooth paste. Now gradually whisk in the milk, followed by the melted butter. Finally mix in the golden syrup, then leave the batter to rest for 20 minutes.

2 Heat a heavy-bottomed frying pan or a flat griddle pan and lightly oil it with a wad of paper towel dipped in sunflower oil. Drop spoonfuls of the batter into the pan and cook over a low to medium heat until bubbles appear on the top. Flip over and cook the other side. Be careful not to have the heat too high otherwise the drop scones will start to burn. You can keep them warm, wrapped loosely in a tea towel on a warm plate, while you cook the rest. Serve with butter and jam, honey or syrup.

drop scone variations

Blueberry Drop Scones – Add 5 ounces blueberries to the mixture.

Walnut Drop Scones – Add a handful of chopped walnuts to the mixture.

VEGETABLE TEMPURA WITH CUCUMBER AND GINGER PICKLE

This is a very light batter. Using soda water aerates the mixture, giving a delicate, crisp coating.

Serves 4

2 zucchini

1 eggplant

a few spears of broccoli

1 sweet potato

12 snow peas or snap peas

12 asparagus spears

12 green beans

sunflower oil for deep-frying

For the pickle:

1 cucumber, peeled and very finely sliced, preferably on a mandoline

1¼-inch piece of fresh ginger, very finely sliced

3½ teaspoons salt

5 teaspoons white wine vinegar

5 teaspoons superfine sugar

For the batter:

5 ounces self-rising flour

2.5 ounces cornstarch

1 egg

1¼ cups soda water

sea salt and black pepper

1 First prepare the vegetables. Cut the zucchini into large batons. Cut the eggplant into 1 1/2-inch cubes and score the skin in a criss-cross pattern. Divide the broccoli into small florets. Peel the sweet potato and cut it into wedges about 1 1/2 inches long and 1/4 inch thick. The peas, asparagus and green beans simply need trimming. Spread out all the vegetables on a tray and make sure they are dry.

2 For the pickle, put the cucumber and ginger in a colander, sprinkle with the salt and leave for 30 minutes, then pat dry. Put the pieces into a bowl, mix with the vinegar and sugar, then drain.

3 To make the batter, put the flour and cornstarch into a bowl and mix well, then make a well in the center. Add the egg and whisk in with a balloon whisk to make a thick paste. Gradually whisk in the soda water. Season with salt and pepper and then pour through a fine sieve.

4 Heat some sunflower oil to 340°F in a deep-fat fryer or a large, deep saucepan. Dip the vegetables in the batter, allow the excess to drip back into the bowl, then fry them in batches for about 3 minutes, turning halfway through. When they are done, they should be tender inside and crisp and golden on the outside. Drain on paper towel and serve straight away, with the pickle.

TOAD IN THE HOLE

This is the ultimate comfort food. Children love it and it is very easy to make. I sometimes serve it with a tomato chili relish. It's worth buying really good sausages here.

Serves 4

8 pork sausages

1 tablespoon goose fat or sunflower oil

Yorkshire Pudding batter (see right), made with 5 ounces all-purpose flour, a pinch of salt, 3 medium eggs, 1¼ cups whole milk and 1 tablespoon chopped thyme

sea salt and black pepper

1 quantity of Onion Marmalade (see page 215), to serve

1 Put the sausages in a large roasting pan and place in an oven preheated to 375°F. Cook for about 30 minutes, until browned all over, then remove from the pan.

2 Turn the oven temperature up to 425°F. Add the goose fat or oil to the pan and put it back in the oven for about 5 minutes to get really hot. Season the batter well with salt and pepper.

3 Return the sausages to the pan and pour in the batter. It should be sizzling. Place in the oven and cook for 20 minutes, then reduce the temperature to 375°F and cook for 5 minutes longer, until well risen and browned. Serve immediately, with the Onion Marmalade.

YORKSHIRE PUDDING

This recipe should give you the biggest Yorkshire puddings you have ever had. The large quantity of eggs gives it a huge rise. Make sure you get the fat really hot before adding the cold batter, to give it plenty of oomph.

Serves 6

3.5 ounces all-purpose flour

a pinch of salt

3 medium eggs

¾ cup whole milk

2 ounces drippings or sunflower oil

1 Sift the flour and salt into a bowl and make a well in the center. Break in the eggs and mix well, drawing in the flour from the sides. Gradually beat in the milk, then continue to beat until smooth. Cover and leave to rest for 1 hour.

2 Put the drippings or sunflower oil in a baking pan about 9 inches square, or in a 6-cup Yorkshire pudding tin or a 10–12-cup muffin tin. Place in an oven preheated to 425°F until smoking hot. Pour in the batter and return to the hot oven for 20 minutes or until risen and golden. Serve immediately.

SOUFFLÉS

Soufflés are one of the easiest things you can cook — but if you don't know the rules they are one of the most difficult. When you get it right, it is so exciting and everybody will be impressed. Once you've mastered the technique, soufflés are endlessly versatile, and you can make up your own variations. Although they feel like a treat, they are actually not expensive to make at all.

Gruyère is the traditional choice for a cheese soufflé and gives a wonderful flavor, but a mature Cheddar works very well too.

CHEESE SOUFFLÉ

SERVES 8 AS A STARTER,
4 AS A MAIN COURSE

2 tablespoons unsalted butter, plus some very soft unsalted butter for greasing

2 ounces Parmesan cheese, freshly grated, plus extra for coating the dish

1 ounce all-purpose flour

¾ cup whole milk

4 ounces Gruyère or strong Cheddar cheese, finely grated

a good pinch of cayenne pepper

4 egg yolks

6 egg whites

sea salt and white pepper

1 First grease the inside of an 8- to 9-cup soufflé dish (or eight ¾- to 1-cup ramekins) with soft butter.

2 Sprinkle some grated Parmesan all over, turning the dish to coat the sides and tipping out any excess.

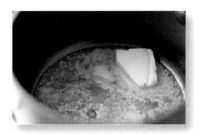

3 To make a roux, melt the 2 tablespoons butter in a small pan.

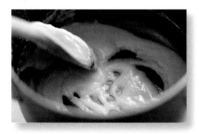

4 Add the flour and cook, stirring, over a low heat for 30 seconds, without letting it brown.

5 Gradually pour in the milk, stirring all the time and making sure there are no lumps.

6 Bring to a simmer and cook gently for 1 minute.

7 Remove from the heat, add the Parmesan and Gruyère or Cheddar cheese and stir until completely melted.

8 Add the cayenne pepper and season very generously with salt and white pepper.

9 Leave the mixture until it is just warm, then add the egg yolks and mix well.

10 Put the egg whites in a large, very clean bowl with a pinch of salt. Whisk until they form soft peaks.

11 Put the cheesy béchamel mixture into a large bowl and whisk in about a third of the egg whites. Gently fold in the rest with a large metal spoon, trying to keep as much air in the mixture as possible. Fill the soufflé dish or ramekins about three-quarters full. Place on a hot baking sheet in an oven preheated to 375°F and bake for about 25 minutes for a large soufflé, 10–12 minutes for small ones. The soufflé is ready when it is well risen, firm around the edges but soft and creamy in the center; it should have a slight wobble. Take the soufflé straight to the table and make sure everyone is ready, so they see it in all its glory before it begins to fall.

cheese soufflé variations

Goat Cheese Soufflé – follow the recipe on pages 94–95, dusting the dishes with 6 tablespoons of finely chopped walnuts instead of Parmesan. Omit the Gruyère or Cheddar and instead stir 5 ounces crumbled goat cheese into the béchamel. Season with cayenne, salt and pepper. Fold in the whisked egg whites as above. Half fill the soufflé dish with the mixture, then place 3.5 ounces crumbled goat cheese in the middle. Top with the remaining soufflé mixture and bake as described above.

Wild Mushroom Soufflé – heat 3½ tablespoons unsalted butter in a large frying pan, add 9 ounces roughly chopped mixed wild mushrooms and sauté for about 10 minutes, until tender. Add 1 finely chopped garlic clove and 1 tablespoon finely chopped thyme and season well. Cool slightly, then transfer to a food processor and whiz to a rough purée; don't make it too smooth, as it needs to have some texture. Prepare the soufflé as on pages 94–95, using 2.5 ounces Gruyère cheese and adding the mushroom mixture after stirring in the Parmesan.

TIPS AND IDEAS

■ The butter for greasing the dish must be very soft and creamy rather than melted, so it stays on.

■ Parmesan makes a delicious coating for a cheese or spinach soufflé. For coating a sweet soufflé, you can dust the dish with sugar, grated chocolate or finely chopped nuts.

■ The flavoring of the base mixture must be strong and well seasoned because it will be diluted by the egg whites.

■ Make sure the bowl for the egg whites is completely clean and grease free or the whites won't whisk properly.

■ Don't overwhip the egg whites or you will lose the rise in your soufflé – they should be stiff but not dry.

■ If you don't have a large soufflé dish, you can use whatever ovenproof container you have at hand – a cake pan, a casserole dish, a sauté pan. Your soufflé will still rise spectacularly and taste wonderful. Be sure not to fill the dish more than three-quarters full (if you have a little mixture left over, pour it into a small dish and cook it separately).

■ It's a fallacy to say you can't open the oven when cooking a soufflé – what you must not do is bang the oven door.

■ Surprisingly, soufflés can be frozen: simply assemble in the dish, as above, then freeze. Cook from frozen, adding a few minutes to the cooking time.

■ You can make your soufflé base in advance. Cook it up to the end of step 6 (to just before adding the cheese) and store in the fridge, where it will keep for a couple of days. When you are ready to make your soufflé, warm up the base and continue as on page 95.

SMOKED HADDOCK SOUFFLÉ

I love the flavor of smoked haddock and this is a wonderful way to use it.
It's a very robust flavor, which is exactly what a soufflé needs.

Serves 8 as a starter,
4 as a main course

16 ounces undyed smoked haddock

milk to cover

2 tablespoons unsalted butter, plus some very
soft butter for greasing

about 2½ tablespoons freshly grated
Parmesan cheese

1 ounce all-purpose flour

2½ tablespoons grated Cheddar cheese

4 egg yolks

6 egg whites

sea salt and black pepper

1 Put the haddock into a gratin dish, season with salt and pepper, then pour over enough milk just to cover. Cover with foil and place in an oven preheated to 350°F. Bake for 20 minutes, until the haddock is just cooked. Leave until the fish is cool enough to handle, then remove it from the milk (reserve the milk for making the roux), remove the skin and any bones and flake the flesh.

2 Grease the inside of an 8- to 9-cup soufflé dish (or eight 3/4- to 1-cup ramekins) with soft butter, then sprinkle the grated Parmesan all over, turning the dish to coat the sides and tipping out any excess.

3 Melt the 2 tablespoons butter in a small pan, add the flour and cook, stirring, over a low heat for 30 seconds, without letting it brown. Gradually pour in 3/4 cup of the reserved milk from cooking the haddock, stirring all the time and making sure there are no lumps. Bring to a simmer and cook gently for 1 minute. Remove from the heat, add the cheese and stir until melted. Season generously with salt and pepper. Leave the mixture until it is just warm, then add the egg yolks and mix well. Finally, fold in the smoked haddock.

4 Put the egg whites in a large, very clean bowl with a pinch of salt. Whisk until they form soft peaks, then fold them into the soufflé mixture and fill the soufflé dish or ramekins about three-quarters full and bake as described on page 95.

SPINACH AND ARUGULA SOUFFLÉ

A deliciously fresh-flavoured soufflé, perfect for vegetarians. Make sure the spinach and arugula are very dry when you add them to the soufflé base, so they don't dilute it.

**Serves 8 as a starter,
4 as a main course**

6 tablespoons unsalted butter, plus some very soft butter for greasing

3½ tablespoons freshly grated Parmesan cheese

1 ounce all-purpose flour

¾ cup whole milk

2½ tablespoons grated Gruyère cheese

9 ounces fresh spinach

2 ounces arugula

4 egg yolks

6 egg whites

sea salt and black pepper

1 First grease the inside of an 8- to 9-cup soufflé dish (or eight 3/4- to 1-cup ramekins) with soft butter, then sprinkle 2 tablespoons of the grated Parmesan all over, turning the dish to coat the sides and tipping out any excess.

2 Melt 2 tablespoons of the butter in a small pan, add the flour and cook, stirring, over a low heat for 30 seconds, without letting it brown. Gradually pour in the milk, stirring all the time and making sure there are no lumps. Bring to a simmer and cook gently for 1 minute. Remove from the heat and add the Gruyère and the remaining Parmesan, stirring thoroughly until the cheese has melted.

3 Heat the remaining butter in a large pan, add the spinach and arugula and cook gently until wilted. Drain very thoroughly and squeeze out as much liquid as possible, so that the sauce doesn't become too sloppy to take the egg white. Chop the arugula and spinach finely, or process briefly in a food processor.

4 To assemble the soufflé, spoon the béchamel sauce into a large mixing bowl and stir in the egg yolks, followed by the spinach and arugula mixture and season with salt and pepper.

5 Put the egg whites in a large, very clean bowl with a pinch of salt. Whisk until they form soft peaks, then fold them into the soufflé mixture and fill the soufflé dish or ramekins about three-quarters full and bake as described on page 95.

TWICE-BAKED CHEESE SOUFFLÉS

The beauty of these twice-baked soufflés is they can be made way in advance and given their final baking just before serving.

Serves 8

2 tablespoons unsalted butter, plus very soft butter for greasing

2 ounces Parmesan cheese, freshly grated, for dusting

1 ounce all-purpose flour

1 teaspoon English mustard powder

¾ cup whole milk

a pinch of grated nutmeg

a pinch of cayenne pepper

3.5 ounces Gruyère cheese, grated

2 ounces strong Cheddar cheese, grated

6 egg yolks

8 egg whites

1⅔ cups heavy cream (optional)

sea salt and black pepper

1 Grease the inside of 8 large ramekin dishes (3/4–1 cup in capacity) with soft butter and sprinkle with grated Parmesan, turning the dishes to coat the sides evenly.

2 Now make the roux. Melt the butter in a small pan, add the flour and mustard and cook, stirring, over a low heat for 1 minute. Gradually, add the milk, stirring all the time and making sure there are no lumps. Bring to a simmer and cook gently for 2 minutes. Add the nutmeg, cayenne, Gruyère and Cheddar and season generously with salt and pepper. Leave until the mixture is just warm, then mix in the egg yolks.

3 Whisk the egg whites in a large bowl with a pinch of salt until they form soft peaks. Put the cheesy béchamel mixture into a large bowl and whisk in about a third of the egg whites. Gently fold in the rest with a large metal spoon, trying to keep as much air in the mixture as possible.

4 Fill the ramekins with the mixture, smooth the tops with a spatula and run your thumb around the inside rim of each one (this helps the mixture to rise).

5 Put the dishes on a baking tray and transfer to an oven preheated to 375°F. Cook for 10–12 minutes or until well risen and firm around the edges but still soft in the center. Remove from the oven and leave to cool, then run a knife around the edge of each soufflé and turn them out of the dishes. At this stage they can be put into the fridge for later or they can be frozen.

6 When ready to reheat, divide the cream, if using, between 8 individual gratin dishes (or pour it into one large gratin dish) and put a soufflé into each one. If you don't want to use the cream, just put the soufflés into generously buttered dishes. Put into an oven preheated to 375°F for 10 minutes or until light and puffy. Serve immediately.

CRAB SOUFFLÉ

This is delicious, and if you can get hold of lovely fresh crab it will be even better. Otherwise, use good pasteurized crab, available in packets.

**Serves 8 as a starter,
4 as a main course**

2 tablespoons unsalted butter, plus some very soft butter for greasing

about 2½ tablespoons freshly grated Parmesan cheese

1 ounce all-purpose flour

¾ cup whole milk

1 teaspoon tomato paste

a good pinch of cayenne pepper

2½ tablespoons grated Gruyère cheese

4 egg yolks

11 ounces crab meat (⅔ white meat, ⅓ brown)

2½ teaspoons brandy (optional)

6 egg whites

sea salt and black pepper

1 First grease the inside of a 8- to 9-cup soufflé dish (or eight 3/4- to 1-cup ramekins) with soft butter, then sprinkle the grated Parmesan all over, turning the dish to coat the sides and tipping out any excess.

2 Melt the 2 tablespoons butter in a small pan, add the flour and cook, stirring, over a low heat for 30 seconds, without letting it brown. Gradually pour in the milk, stirring all the time and making sure there are no lumps. Bring to a simmer and cook gently for 1 minute. Stir in the tomato paste, cayenne and Gruyère cheese. Mix well and season with salt. Allow to cool a little, then stir in the egg yolks and crab meat. Mix again and add the brandy, if using. Check the seasoning.

3 Put the egg whites in a large, very clean bowl with a pinch of salt. Whisk until they form soft peaks, then fold them into the soufflé mixture and fill the soufflé dish or ramekins about three-quarters full and bake as described on page 95.

GRAND MARNIER SOUFFLÉ

This is one of my favourite soufflés. Patience is needed here, as you have to reduce the orange juice sufficiently to get a very concentrated flavor.

Serves 4–6

very soft unsalted butter for greasing

1.5 ounces superfine sugar, plus extra for dusting

1⅔ cups fresh orange juice

7 ounces Crème Pâtissière (see page 228)

2½ tablespoons Grand Marnier

6 egg whites

confectioner's sugar for dusting

1 Butter 4–6 ramekins, 3/4–1 cup in capacity, and sprinkle with superfine sugar, turning the dishes to coat the sides and tipping out any excess.

2 Put the orange juice into a small saucepan, bring to a boil and boil until reduced to 3 tablespoons; this gives a really intense flavor. Stir it into the crème pâtissière along with the Grand Marnier.

3 Put the egg whites in a large, very clean bowl and whisk until they form fairly firm peaks. Add 1.5 ounces of superfine sugar and continue whisking for 30 seconds. Whisk a third of this meringue into the crème pâtissière to loosen it, then gently fold in the rest with a large metal spoon, trying to keep as much air in the mixture as possible.

4 Fill the dishes with the mixture, place on a hot baking sheet in an oven preheated to 375°F and bake for 10 minutes, until the soufflés are well risen, lightly colored and have a slight wobble in the center. Dust with confectioner's sugar and serve immediately.

HOT CHOCOLATE SOUFFLÉ

This uses chocolate and cocoa powder for a great depth of flavor.

Serves 4–6

very soft unsalted butter for greasing

2 ounces good-quality cocoa powder, sifted, plus extra for dusting

7 ounces Crème Pâtissière (see page 228)

3.5 ounces plain chocolate, very finely chopped

6 egg whites

1.5 ounces superfine sugar

confectioner's sugar for dusting

1 Butter 4–6 ramekins, 3/4–1 cup in capacity, and dust with cocoa powder, turning the dishes to coat the sides and tipping out any excess.

2 Gently reheat the crème pâtissière, if necessary, and add the chocolate and sifted cocoa powder. Stir until melted and well combined.

3 Put the egg whites in a large, very clean bowl and whisk to fairly firm peaks. Add the superfine sugar and continue whisking for 30 seconds. Whisk a third of this meringue into the chocolate crème pâtissière to loosen it, then gently fold in the rest with a large metal spoon, trying to keep as much air in the mixture as possible.

4 Fill the dishes with the mixture, place on a hot baking sheet in an oven preheated to 375°F and bake for 10 minutes, until the soufflés are well risen and have a slight wobble in the centre. Dust with confectioner's sugar and serve immediately.

COLD LEMON SOUFFLÉ

This is a wonderful way to impress your guests, as you tie paper round the dishes, then overfill them with the soufflé mixture and leave to set. When you remove the paper, it looks just like a perfectly risen soufflé.

Serves 4–6

2 gelatin sheets

1 quantity of Crème Pâtissière (see page 228)

juice and grated zest of 3 lemons

3 egg whites

1 ounce superfine sugar

⅔ cup heavy cream

1 Take 4–6 small ramekins (or one soufflé dish, about 3 1/2 cups in capacity) and wrap a piece of wax paper firmly around each one; it should come about 2 1/2 inches above the rim. You can tie it on with string or use tape.

2 Soak the gelatin sheets in a shallow dish of cold water for 10–15 minutes, until soft. Make the crème patissière and measure 7 ounces (you won't need the rest for this recipe). Squeeze the water from the gelatin sheets, add them to the hot crème pâtissière and stir until dissolved. Now add the lemon juice and zest, mix well and leave to cool completely. Strain the mixture through a sieve.

3 Whisk the egg whites with the superfine sugar until they form soft peaks. In a separate bowl, whip the cream until it forms soft peaks. Mix a third of the cream into the lemon mixture, then gently fold in the rest. Finally fold the whisked whites into the lemon mixture, using a large metal spoon and being careful not to knock out the air.

4 Transfer the mixture to the ramekins or a large soufflé dish, overfilling them so it comes about 1 inch above the rim. Chill for about 3 hours, until set. Carefully peel off the paper before serving.

TERRINES
and
PÂTÉS

These are not usually considered an essential part of everyone's repertoire but I feel strongly that they should be. It's a wonderful way of feeding a lot of people. A good pâté or terrine will keep in the fridge for ages, and terrines in particular are fun to prepare and look so impressive. Let it be your secret that terrines are actually very simple to make. There are no real cooking skills to master, it is just a question of layering the ingredients in the dish.

This terrine is very good with a few lightly dressed salad leaves (see pages 12–13) and some chutney. Use a 9 x 5 x 3-inch terrine dish or loaf tin.

Chicken, pork and pistachio
TERRINE

SERVES ABOUT 12

3 large skinless, boneless chicken breasts, cut into long strips about ¼ inch thick

15 very thin slices of Parma ham

1¾ pounds pork belly, finely minced

3 garlic cloves, crushed to a paste

1 egg

1 teaspoon Chinese five-spice powder

2½ tablespoons brandy

2 handfuls of pistachio nuts

sea salt and black pepper

1 Put the chicken strips into a dish.

2 Season with salt and pepper and set aside while you prepare the rest of the filling.

3 Line the terrine dish with Parma ham. Make sure there are no gaps and let the ends overhang the dish – save 2 pieces for the top.

4 Put the minced pork and all the remaining ingredients into a bowl, mix and season well – this mixture will help your terrine hold together.

5 Spread one third of the pork mixture evenly over the bottom of the lined terrine dish.

6 Arrange half of the chicken on top.

7 Repeat these layers, then finish with a final layer of the pork mixture.

8 Fold the Parma ham over the top and add the 2 reserved slices, if necessary, to cover the filling completely.

9 Cover the terrine with foil.

10 Put a wad of wax paper or a folded newspaper into the roasting pan; sit the terrine dish on top.

11 Pour in cold water to come three-quarters of the way up the dish. Place in an oven preheated to 375°F and cook for 20 minutes.

12 Turn the oven down to 275°F and cook for 1½ hours. Use a meat thermometer to check if it is done – it should register 150–160°F.

13 Another way to check is to press gently with your finger: the juices should run clear and the terrine should be fairly firm but still with a little give.

14 Remove from the oven, make little holes in the top with a skewer.

15 Then put a weight on top such as several cans or another terrine dish and leave to cool. Leave overnight in the fridge, still weighted down.

16 To remove the terrine from the dish, put a roll of plastic wrap behind a board and pull the plastic wrap over the board. Do not cut it at this point.

17 Turn out the terrine on to the plastic wrap; remove any excess jelly.

18 Start wrapping the terrine using the roll behind the board as leverage. When it is wrapped in 7 or 8 layers, cut the cling film and chill the terrine again. To serve, slice the terrine through the plastic wrap with a very sharp, thin knife, using a sawing motion. This helps each slice hold together. Peel off the plastic wrap and serve.

TIPS AND IDEAS

■ The basic question to consider when making a terrine is how it is going to hold together when it is turned out. You need to choose your 'glue': a finely minced or ground meat, such as the pork in the recipe above, a jelly, a fish mousse or just by pressing it. Once you have your chosen glue, anything goes in terms of the main ingredients.

■ If you don't want anything surrounding your terrine, line the dish with 3 layers of plastic wrap instead, letting the sides hang over the edges of the dish.

■ To check the seasoning, make a patty with a tiny amount of the ground meat mixture and fry it. Taste and adjust the seasoning of the rest of your mixture if necessary.

■ When assembling a terrine, you get a more even effect if you shred the ingredients rather than cutting them into chunks.

■ The terrine will keep for 5 days, tightly wrapped in the fridge. It also freezes well. If you don't want to use all the terrine, you can cut it in half, wrap in plastic wrap as above and store one half in the freezer.

terrine variations

Chicken, Pork and Walnut Terrine
– dice 4 ounces walnuts, sauté very
lightly and use in the recipe on pages
106–108 instead of the pistachios.

Game Terrine – replace the Parma
ham in the recipe on pages 106–108
with 15 slices of bacon. For the ground
meat, mix 1¼ pounds minced venison
shoulder, or minced mixed game,
such as pheasant and rabbit, with 11
ounces minced pork fat, 5 tablespoons
of port, 1 teaspoon of ground mace,
2½ tablespoons of juniper berries and
2 finely chopped garlic cloves. Omit
the chicken breasts and instead cut 2
skinned pheasant breasts into ½-inch
dice, season well and add to the minced
game mixture. Put the mixture into the
terrine dish, fold the bacon ends over the
top, then cover with foil and cook as for
the Chicken, Pork and Pistachio Terrine.
Turn out and wrap in plastic wrap in the
same way.

■ Substitute rabbit, guinea fowl or
pheasant for the chicken.

■ Substitute walnuts for the pistachios.

■ Add 2½ tablespoons of chopped
mixed chives and parsley to the ground
meat.

■ Line the terrine dish with bacon, or
blanched spinach or chard leaves
(first removing the stalks), instead of
Parma ham.

PORK AND RABBIT PÂTÉ

*This is so easy to make – you just mix everything
together. Do make sure it's properly seasoned
though. It makes all the difference between a bland
dish and an unforgettable one.*

Serves 8

15 thin bacon slices

the meat of 2 rabbits (you can ask your
butcher to skin and bone them for you)

25 ounces pork belly, finely minced

3 garlic cloves, finely chopped

2½ teaspoons dried thyme

1 teaspoon dried rosemary

3.5 ounces unsalted butter, melted

½ cup brandy

3 bay leaves

sea salt and black pepper

1 Line a large, oval pâté dish, about 9 inches long (or
an ovenproof dish) with the bacon, letting the slices
overhang the top.

2 Put the rabbit meat in a food processor and process
roughly, then transfer it to a bowl. Add the pork,
garlic, thyme, rosemary, melted butter, brandy and
plenty of salt and pepper and mix well. Cook a small
patty to test the seasoning (see Tips and Ideas, page
108). Put the mixture into the prepared dish and fold
over the bacon to cover it. Top with the bay leaves
and cover with foil.

3 Put the dish into a roasting pan containing a
wad of wax paper or a folded newspaper, pour in
enough cold water to come about three-quarters of
the way up the sides of the dish, then place in an
oven preheated to 300°F. Cook for 1 1/2 hours, until
the juices run clear when a knife is inserted in the
center. You can also check with a meat thermometer,
which should register 150–160°F. Remove and leave
to cool, then leave overnight in the fridge before
serving. It's delicious with crusty bread.

HAM HOCK, CHICKEN AND PARMA HAM TERRINE

This looks complicated but I promise you it's not. You have to add everything while it's still warm, and then leave it to set in the fridge. The gelatin isn't absolutely essential but it will ensure that the terrine holds together rather than leaving it to chance.

Serves about 12

15 very thin slices of Parma ham

2 ham hocks

1 bay leaf

2 sprigs of parsley

2 sprigs of thyme

1 onion, quartered

1 celery stalk, chopped

1 tablespoon olive oil

2 shallots, finely chopped

8 gelatin sheets

3 chicken breasts

sea salt and black pepper

1 Line a 9 x 5 x 3-inch terrine dish or loaf pan with 3 layers of plastic wrap, letting it overhang the sides. Then line it with the Parma ham, making sure there are no gaps and letting the ends overhang the top of the dish – allow 2 extra pieces for the top just in case you don't have enough to fold over.

2 Put the ham hocks, herbs, onion and celery into a saucepan, add enough water to cover and bring to the boil. Reduce the heat and cook at a low simmer for 3 hours, topping up the water if the level gets too low. The meat should be very tender. Remove the hocks from the cooking liquid, reserving the liquid, and shred all the meat from the bones, discarding the skin and gristle. Put the meat into a bowl, season well and keep warm. Heat the oil in a small pan, add the shallots and cook for about 5 minutes, until softened. Add the shallots to the shredded ham.

3 Put the gelatin in a large shallow dish full of cold water and leave to soak for about 10 minutes, until soft and pliable. Pour 1 1/4 cups of the stock from cooking the ham into a small pan and heat until very hot but not boiling. Gently squeeze out the excess water from the gelatin, add to the hot ham stock and stir to dissolve. Keep warm.

4 Season the chicken breasts with salt and pepper and wrap each one in plastic wrap. Place in a steamer and steam for 7 minutes, until cooked through. Remove from the steamer while still warm and shred the chicken.

5 Put a layer of warm ham in the bottom of the terrine, pour a little of the gelatin ham stock over, then add a layer of chicken, then more ham, then another layer of chicken, being sure to pour in a little of the ham stock with each layer. Finish with ham, pour in the last of the stock, then bring the Parma ham over and make sure the meat is completely covered. Bring over the plastic wrap and make 3 holes down each side with a sharp knife so the juices can escape. Put a heavy weight on top, such as another terrine dish or, if you are using a loaf pan, another loaf pan and a couple of cans. Leave in the fridge overnight to set.

6 To turn out the terrine, put a roll of plastic wrap behind a board and pull it over the board as described on page 108. Open the plastic wrap covering the top of the terrine and invert the terrine upside down on to the plastic wrap on the board. Gently pull the cooking plastic wrap from the terrine and wrap up as instructed on page 108.

SALMON AND SOLE TERRINE

This terrine is slightly tricky because you need to be careful not to over process the cream, or it can separate. Other than that, everything is straightforward, and it's great fun to build up the layers in the dish.

Serves about 12

5 ounces large spinach leaves

2 tablespoons unsalted butter, melted

2½ tablespoons finely chopped chives

2½ tablespoons finely chopped parsley

2½ tablespoons finely chopped chervil or tarragon

3 large lemon sole fillets, skinned

sea salt and black pepper

For the salmon mousse:

14 ounces salmon fillet, skinned

2 small egg whites

1½ cups heavy cream

2½ tablespoons finely chopped parsley

1 Put the spinach leaves in a large pan of boiling salted water, cook for 1 minute, then drain well. Lay the leaves out on kitchen paper to dry.

2 Line a 9 x 5 x 3-inch terrine dish or loaf pan with 4 layers of plastic wrap, making sure they overlap the sides by 4 inches all round. Now line the terrine with the blanched spinach leaves, being careful not to leave any gaps and letting them overhang the edges of the terrine. Carefully brush the spinach with the melted butter and then put the dish into the fridge until needed.

3 Remove any pin bones from the salmon, being very careful to make sure there are no bones left. Put the fish into a processor and whiz until smooth. Add the egg whites and process again to loosen the mixture. Pour in half the cream and pulse until mixed, then add the remainder and pulse again. Transfer the mixture to a bowl. Season well with salt and pepper. Stir in the chopped parsley and place in the fridge.

4 To assemble the terrine, spread the herbs out on a plate and divide the salmon mousse into 3. Arrange a third of the mousse in a layer in the terrine dish, making sure it is level. Dip a lemon sole fillet into the chopped herbs and place it on top of the mousse. You will only need 2 layers of sole, so use the third fillet to fill in the gaps at either end. Add another layer of mousse, then another layer of lemon sole and finally the last layer of mousse. Fold the overlapping spinach over the top, then bring up the plastic wrap and seal. Cover with foil and place in a bain marie (a roasting pan full of water), following the instructions on page 107. Place in an oven preheated to 375°F and bake for 20 minutes. Turn the oven down to 275°F and cook for a further 1 hour 10 minutes. The terrine is done when it is firm to the touch and a skewer inserted in the centre comes out clean; you can also check with a digital cooking thermometer, which should register 150°F. Remove the terrine from the oven and leave to cool, then chill overnight.

5 Unwrap the plastic wrap from the top of the terrine, turn out the terrine on to some clean plastic wrap and remove the old plastic wrap and any residue that has come off during cooking. Wrap the terrine up about 8 times in the new plastic wrap and put it into the fridge until required. Serve cut into slices, accompanied by a little green salad.

PROVENÇAL TERRINE WITH GOAT CHEESE

A fairly time-consuming dish to make but it's well worth it. You have to be very careful when you cut the terrine, as it is delicate and can collapse quite easily. When you layer it in the dish, press down well to compact it.

Serves 8–10

3 large eggplants

extra virgin olive oil

3 red peppers

6 medium zucchini

18 ounces soft, fresh goat cheese

20 basil leaves, shredded

sea salt and black pepper

1 Cut the eggplants lengthwise into slices about 1/4 inch thick, put them in a colander and sprinkle with salt. Leave to drain for 30 minutes, then pat dry. Brush them with oil on both sides and arrange on baking sheets. Season with salt and pepper and place in an oven preheated to 375°F. Bake for about 20 minutes, until tender and golden, turning halfway through.

2 Put the peppers into an ovenproof dish and sprinkle with oil. Bake at the same temperature as the eggplant for 20 minutes or until patched with brown, turning halfway through. Cool slightly and peel off the skin, then remove the seeds and cut the peppers into large, long pieces.

3 Cut the zucchini lengthwise into slices 1/4 inch thick and fry in olive oil until browned on both sides, transferring them to paper towel to soak up excess oil as they are done.

4 Take a 9 x 5 x 3-inch terrine dish or loaf pan and line it with plastic wrap, letting the ends overhang the top of the pan. To assemble the terrine, line the sides of the dish with eggplant, overlapping the slices slightly and letting them overhang the top of the dish. Put a further layer of eggplant on the base. Divide the goat cheese into three and put one portion in a thin layer on top of the eggplant. Add a layer of red pepper and season well. Add another layer of goat cheese, then a layer of basil with the zucchini. Season the zucchini with salt and pepper and add a final layer of goat cheese. Finish off with a layer of eggplant and bring the plastic wrap over the top. Put a heavy weight on top of the terrine and allow to rest overnight in the fridge.

5 To turn out, follow the instructions on page 108, wrapping the terrine in 10 layers of plastic wrap as this one can be difficult to cut.

SMOKED TROUT PÂTÉ

This pâté is unbelievably quick and easy to make. There is no cooking involved whatsoever, yet it makes a perfect dinner-party starter.

Serves 6

1 pound smoked trout fillets, skinned and boned

½ cup crème fraîche

5 ounces cream cheese

1–2½ tablespoons lemon juice

½ teaspoon cayenne pepper

¼ teaspoon ground mace

2½ tablespoons horseradish sauce

2½ tablespoons chopped dill, plus sprigs of dill to garnish

sea salt and black pepper

1 Put the smoked trout, crème fraîche and cream cheese into a food processor and process to a purée. Add 1 tablespoon of the lemon juice, plus the spices and horseradish and process again.

2 Transfer to a bowl and season well, adding more lemon juice if necessary. Mix in the chopped dill, then transfer to 6 small ramekins or one large dish and garnish with dill sprigs. Serve at room temperature, with crusty bread.

CHICKEN LIVER PÂTÉ

There's nothing nicer than chicken liver pâté with a thick slice of whole wheat toast and a bit of pickle on the side.

Serves 8

1¾ pounds chicken livers

1 tablespoon olive oil

2 shallots, finely chopped

2 garlic cloves, finely chopped

5 teaspoons thyme leaves

5 tablespoons cognac

5 ounces unsalted butter

3.5 ounces clarified butter (see page 57) for the top of the pâté

sea salt and black pepper

1 Trim the chicken livers, cutting off all the sinews. Heat the olive oil in a frying pan, add the shallots, garlic and thyme and cook until softened. Remove from the pan and set aside. Cook the chicken livers in the same pan over a medium heat until pale brown on the outside and just pink inside. Do this in batches, as if you try to do them all at once they will braise rather than fry. Make sure the livers aren't touching each other as they cook.

2 Put the cooked livers with the shallot mixture. Add the cognac to the pan and cook for a minute, stirring and scraping the base of the pan with a wooden spoon to deglaze. When the cognac has reduced to 1 tablespoon, return the chicken livers and shallots to the pan, mix well and season with salt and plenty of black pepper. Remove from the heat and allow to cool. Now put the mixture into a food processor with the butter and process until smooth. Check the seasoning and adjust if necessary. Transfer to an earthenware dish, cover the surface with plastic wrap and refrigerate for at least 4 hours, until set. Pour over the clarified butter and put back in the fridge for 1 hour. Serve the pâté with toast or crusty brown bread. It will keep for about 5 days in the fridge and freezes very well.

RICE

Rice is such a useful cupboard ingredient. If you
have a packet of rice, you can almost conjure up
something out of nothing. But it's surprisingly
delicate and needs to be treated with care,
whether you are making a risotto, a pilaf,
a pudding or just plain boiled rice. In this
chapter you will find all the tips you need for
successful rice dishes.

I tend to cook risottos more slowly that most books recommend, stirring all the time, which gives perfectly cooked rice and a lovely creamy texture.

HERB RISOTTO

SERVES 4

4¼ cups of chicken stock (see pages 30–31) or vegetable stock (see page 35)

3½ tablespoons unsalted butter

1 onion, finely chopped

1 leek, finely chopped

11 ounces risotto rice

½ cup white wine (optional)

2 ounces Parmesan cheese, freshly grated

2½ tablespoons finely chopped parsley

2½ tablespoons finely chopped cilantro

5 tablespoons finely chopped chives

5 tablespoons heavy cream

sea salt and black pepper

 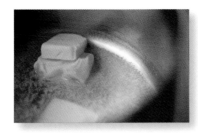 

1 Pour the stock into a pan and bring to a simmer. Keep over a gentle heat while you make the risotto.

2 Melt the butter in a heavy-based saucepan.

3 Add the onion and leek.

4 Stir, then cover and cook gently until soft but not colored.

5 Add the rice and stir until well coated with the butter.

6 Pour in the white wine, if using, and stir until it has been completely absorbed by the rice.

7 Start adding the hot stock a ladleful at a time, stirring continuously.

8 Make sure each addition is absorbed before adding the next ladleful – the rice should be crying out for liquid before you add more.

9 Repeat until you have added all the stock – it should take 25–30 minutes and the mixture should be at a gentle simmer throughout.

10 At the end, the rice should be cooked through but still a little *al dente*.

11 Stir in the Parmesan, parsley, cilantro and 2 tablespoons of the chives.

12 Season well with salt and pepper and gently stir in the cream. Sprinkle with the remaining chives and serve immediately.

risotto variations

Seafood and Saffron Risotto – cut 4 large scallops and 8 large raw shrimp horizontally in half and cut 2 medium squid into rings. Brown the seafood in olive oil in a large frying pan, in batches, adding 2 finely chopped garlic cloves to the last batch. Return all the seafood to the pan and season well. Make the risotto as on pages 118–119, adding a large pinch of saffron strands to the stock and omitting the herbs. Stir the seafood into the risotto and sprinkle with chopped parsley.

Butternut Squash Risotto – peel 1 pound butternut squash and cut it into ½-inch dice. Cook it gently in 4 tablespoons butter in a frying pan for about 40 minutes, until tender but not browned. Season well. Cook the risotto as on pages 118–119, increasing the Parmesan to 3.5 ounces. Stir in the cooked squash and garnish with chopped dill.

Wild Mushroom Risotto – slice 18 ounces mixed wild mushrooms. Melt 6 tablespoons butter in a large, non-stick frying pan, add the mushrooms and cook gently until softened. Make the risotto as on pages 118–119, omitting the herbs and increasing the Parmesan to 3.5 ounces. Serve sprinkled with 5 tablespoons of chopped parsley.

TIPS AND IDEAS

■ You can make risotto several hours in advance if you cook the rice to the *al dente* stage and then transfer it to a tray or shallow dish and leave to cool. When you are ready to serve, return the risotto to the pan, bring up to heat and stir in more stock until you have the right consistency.

■ It is important to use Italian risotto rice. Its high starch content gives the risotto its creamy texture. My favourite type is Carnaroli, but other readily available varieties are Arborio and Vialone Nano.

■ If you run out of stock before the rice is fully cooked, add hot water instead – but not too much.

■ Adding Parmesan and cream at the end enriches a risotto and helps to bind it together. Instead of cream, you can also beat in a generous knob of butter.

■ If you can count the grains in your mouth when eating risotto, that means it is perfectly cooked. If it is overcooked, the grains will merge into a mush.

■ Use leftover risotto to make rice balls (see page 124) or to stuff vegetables such as roasted peppers and eggplants.

BOILING RICE

To cook plain basmati rice, tip the rice into a sieve and rinse it under cold running water, then drain well. Put it into a pan, add enough cold water to come 1/2 inch above the rice and bring to a boil. Cover the pan, reduce the heat to as low as possible and cook for 8 minutes. Turn off the heat and leave, with the lid on, for another 10 minutes. Fluff the rice up gently with a fork – you will have perfect boiled rice.

MUSSEL RISOTTO

If you can't think what to cook, risotto always comes up trumps. I'm very fond of a lovely seafood risotto and this is one of the best.

Serves 4

2 pounds mussels

about 3¾ cups fish stock (see page 35)

2 shallots, finely chopped

3½ tablespoons unsalted butter

1 onion, finely chopped

1 leek, finely chopped

11 ounces risotto rice

½ cup white wine (optional)

sea salt and black pepper

5 tablespoons roughly chopped flat-leaf parsley, to garnish

1 Scrub the mussels under cold running water and remove their 'beards'. Discard any open mussels that don't close when tapped on the work surface.

2 Put 2 cups of the fish stock into a large saucepan, add the shallots and bring to a boil. Add the mussels, cover the pan and steam over high heat for 3–4 minutes, shaking the pan occasionally, until they open. Remove the mussels from the saucepan, discarding any that have refused to open, and strain the cooking juices through a fine sieve into a bowl. When the mussels are cool enough to handle, set 20 aside for garnish, then remove the rest from their shells. Make up the reserved cooking liquid to 4 1/4 cups with more fish stock, pour it into a pan and bring to a simmer. Keep over a gentle heat while you make the risotto.

3 To make the risotto, melt the butter in a heavy-bottomed saucepan, add the onion and leek, then cover and cook gently until soft but not colored. Add the rice and stir until well coated with the butter. Pour in the white wine, if using, and stir until it has been completely absorbed by the rice.

4 Start adding the hot stock a ladleful at a time, stirring continuously and making sure each addition is absorbed before adding the next ladleful. It should take 25–30 minutes to add all the stock and the mixture should be at a gentle simmer throughout. At the end, the rice should be cooked through but still a little *al dente*. Fold in the shelled mussels, then gently add the ones in their shells. Adjust the seasoning, sprinkle with the parsley and serve.

HAZELNUT AND TALEGGIO RISOTTO

Taleggio was one of the first Italian cheeses I ever tried and it remains one of my favorites. Don't let it melt completely into the risotto — you should be able to see the lumps of cheese in the finished dish.

Serves 4

5 ounces hazelnuts

4¼ cups vegetable stock (see page 35) or chicken stock (see pages 30–31)

4 tablespoons unsalted butter

1 onion, finely chopped

1 small leek, finely chopped

1 celery stalk, finely chopped

1 tablespoon thyme leaves

11 ounces risotto rice

½ cup white wine (optional)

2 ounces Parmesan cheese, freshly grated

½ tablespoon finely chopped rosemary

2 sage leaves, finely chopped

7 ounces Taleggio cheese, cut into small pieces

sea salt and black pepper

2½ tablespoons chopped flat-leaf parsley, to garnish

1 Toast the hazelnuts in a dry frying pan until lightly colored, then tip them into a tea towel and rub them together to remove the skins. Chop them roughly.

2 Pour the stock into a pan and bring to a simmer. Keep over a gentle heat while you make the risotto.

3 Melt the butter in a heavy-bottomed saucepan, add the onion, leek and celery then cover and cook gently until soft but not colored. Add the thyme and the rice and stir until well coated with the butter. Pour in the white wine, if using, and stir until it has been completely absorbed by the rice.

4 Start adding the hot stock a ladleful at a time, stirring continuously and making sure each addition is absorbed before adding the next ladleful. It should take 25–30 minutes to add all the stock and the mixture should be at a gentle simmer throughout. At the end, the rice should be cooked through but still a little *al dente*.

5 Stir in the Parmesan and half the hazelnuts and check the seasoning, then add the rosemary, sage and Taleggio. Serve sprinkled with the remaining chopped hazelnuts and the parsley.

RISI E BISI

If you can get hold of fresh peas in their pods, they are particularly good in this soupy risotto.

Serves 4

2½ tablespoons olive oil

1 small onion, finely chopped

3.5 ounces pancetta, finely diced

6¼ cups chicken stock (see pages 30–31)

7 ounces risotto rice

2¼ pounds fresh peas in their pods, shelled (or use 11 ounces frozen peas)

5 tablespoons freshly grated Parmesan cheese

5 tablespoons finely chopped parsley

sea salt and black pepper

1 Heat the oil in a heavy-bottomed saucepan, add the onion and cook gently until softened. Add the pancetta and cook for 2 minutes. Meanwhile, bring the chicken stock to a boil in a separate pan.

2 Stir the rice into the onion and pancetta mixture, then add half the hot chicken stock. Stir well and simmer until the stock has been absorbed. Pour in the rest of the hot stock and cook for about 20 minutes, until the rice has lost its chalkiness. The mixture should be quite soupy.

3 Add the peas and cook gently for 3 minutes, until they are tender. Stir in the Parmesan and chopped parsley, season well with salt and pepper and serve in soup bowls.

RICE BALLS

Known as 'suppli' in Italy, these little balls are a thrifty and delicious way of using up leftover risotto. Children love them and they make great finger food.

Serves 4

7 ounces leftover risotto

7 ounces ground beef (optional)

2½ teaspoons chopped parsley

2 ounces mozzarella, finely chopped

2 ounces Parmesan cheese, grated

1 egg yolk

3 eggs, lightly beaten

5 ounces fresh breadcrumbs

vegetable oil for deep-frying

sea salt and black pepper

1 Mix the risotto and beef together, stir in the parsley, mozzarella and Parmesan and season well with salt and pepper. Bind with the egg yolk.

2 Shape the mixture into walnut-sized balls. Pour the beaten eggs into a dish and put the breadcrumbs in another. Dip the rice balls into the beaten egg, letting the excess drain off, then roll them in breadcrumbs to coat. Chill for 20 minutes, then repeat the egg and breadcrumb coating.

3 Heat the oil to 340°F in a deep-fat fryer or a large, deep saucepan. Fry the rice balls, in batches, for about 5 minutes, until golden and crisp – be careful not to overcrowd the pan. Drain on paper towels and serve at once.

KEDGEREE

Kedgeree always reminds me of my childhood, especially with lots of parsley added to it.

Serves 4

4 eggs

7 ounces basmati rice

18 ounces smoked haddock fillet

2½ cups whole milk

6 tablespoons unsalted butter

1 onion, finely chopped

7 rounded tablespoons of finely chopped parsley

sea salt and black pepper

1 Boil the eggs for 8 minutes as described on page 72, then drain and refresh in cold water. Remove the shells and set aside.

2 Put the rice in a saucepan, add enough cold water to come 1/2 inch above the rice, then cover with a lid and put over a high heat until it starts to boil. Turn the heat down low and simmer for 10 minutes. Turn the heat off but leave the lid on the pan for 5 minutes.

3 Put the haddock into a large frying pan and pour the milk over it. Bring to a simmer and cook very gently for about 3 minutes, turning the fish over if necessary. Remove from the heat and leave to stand for 3 minutes to complete the cooking, then drain well. When the fish is cool enough to handle, flake the flesh, discarding the skin and any bones, and add to the rice.

4 Heat half the butter in a small pan, add the onion and cook gently until soft. Stir it into the rice with the remaining butter and 3 1/2 tablespoons of the parsley. Cut the eggs into quarters and add to rice, then scatter the parsley over and serve.

PEARL BARLEY AND BLACK GRAPE RISOTTO

I love the colour of the black grapes coming through here. The whole dish ends up pink, and it looks beautiful. It's a wonderful combination of sweet and earthy flavors.

Serves 4

4 tablespoons unsalted butter

1 onion, finely chopped

2 carrots, finely chopped

3 celery stalks, finely chopped

5 ounces pearl barley

2 cups vegetable stock (see page 35)

24 black seedless grapes

⅔ cup heavy cream

2½ tablespoons finely chopped parsley

2½ tablespoons finely chopped chives

2½ tablespoons finely chopped tarragon

sea salt and black pepper

1 Melt the butter in a large saucepan, add the onion, carrots and celery and cook gently until softened.

2 Put the pearl barley in a sieve and rinse under cold running water. Drain well and add to the vegetables. Pour in one third of the stock and cook gently for 5 minutes. Add another third of the stock and continue cooking for 5 minutes. Finally add the rest of the stock and the grapes. Simmer for 20–30 minutes, stirring occasionally and adding a little more stock if it begins to look dry.

3 When the pearl barley is tender, stir in the cream and herbs and cook for 2 minutes longer. Adjust the seasoning and serve.

RICE PILAF

I always use basmati rice for pilafs. It has a delicate, yet deliciously nutty flavor and is easier to cook than other varieties of long grain rice, holding its shape well. When making a pilaf, the trick is to keep it drier than most rice dishes. Add enough stock to come level with the top of the rice.

Serves 6

4 tablespoons unsalted butter

1 carrot, cut into ½-inch dice

1 leek, cut into ½-inch dice

1 celery stalk, cut into ½-inch dice

1 small onion, cut into ½-inch dice

9 ounces basmati rice

about 1⅔ cups hot chicken stock (see pages 30–31) or vegetable stock (see page 35)

sea salt and black pepper

5 tablespoons chopped parsley, to garnish

1 Melt the butter in a large casserole or a small, heavy-bottomed roasting pan, add the vegetables and cook gently for a few minutes, until softened.

2 Add the rice and stir everything together over a low heat for a couple of minutes. Pour in 1 1/4 cups hot stock and then cover the surface of the pilaf with a sheet of buttered wax paper. Place in an oven preheated to 325°F and bake for 25–35 minutes, topping up with hot stock if the mixture dries out too quickly.

3 When the rice is tender and still slightly nutty, take it out of the oven, fluff with a fork and season to taste with salt and pepper. Sprinkle the parsley over and serve.

RICE SALAD WITH TOMATOES, PINE NUTS, RAISINS AND HERBS

Serves 6

2½ tablespoons raisins

11 ounces basmati rice

2½ tablespoons olive oil

2 onions, finely chopped

4 large, vine-ripened tomatoes, skinned deseeded and finely diced (see page 135)

2½ rounded tablespoons pine nuts, lightly toasted in a dry frying pan

2½ rounded tablespoons finely chopped parsley

2½ rounded tablespoons finely chopped mint

1 rounded tablespoon finely chopped chives

sea salt and black pepper

1 Put the raisins in a bowl, pour over enough boiling water to cover generously and leave to soak for 30 minutes. Meanwhile, boil the rice according to the instructions on page 120. Fluff it up with a fork and leave to cool.

2 Heat the oil in a saucepan, add the onions and cook gently until soft. Drain the raisins. Gently stir them into the rice together with the onions, tomatoes, pine nuts and herbs. Mix well and season to taste.

rice pilaf variations

Turkey, Chicken or Lamb Pilaf – simply fold cold leftover turkey, chicken or lamb through the cooked pilaf above.

Seafood Pilaf – sear seafood in olive oil and season well, then add to the cooked pilaf above.

CHESTNUT PILAF

This has the most delicious flavor and makes a wonderful alternative to serve with turkey at Christmas.

Serves 6

6 tablespoons unsalted butter

3 carrots, finely diced

1 onion, finely diced

3.5 ounces vacuum-packed chestnuts

1 teaspoon sugar

2½ teaspoons ground cinnamon

½ teaspoon ground allspice

9 ounces basmati rice

about 1¼ cups chicken stock (see pages 30–31)

sea salt and black pepper

1 Melt the butter in a large casserole or a small, heavy-bottomed roasting pan, add the carrots and onion and cook gently for a few minutes, until softened.

2 Crumble in the chestnuts, then add the sugar and spices and mix well. Add the rice, stir to coat with the butter, then pour in 1 1/4 cups chicken stock and season with salt and pepper. Cover the mixture with a sheet of buttered wax paper, letting it rest on the surface. Transfer to an oven preheated to 325°F and bake for 25–35 minutes, until the rice is just tender, adding more stock if it dries out.

3 Remove the pilaf from the oven, fluff up the rice with a fork and serve straight away.

TURKEY AND ORANGE PILAF

Serves 4

a large pinch of saffron strands

about 1 cup chicken stock (see pages 30–31)

2½ tablespoons sunflower oil

1 large onion, chopped

9 ounces basmati rice

14 ounces cooked turkey meat, preferably from the leg, diced

¼ cup orange juice

1 tablespoon sugar

½ teaspoon crushed cardamom seeds

5 tablespoons flaked almonds, lightly toasted in a dry frying pan

5 tablespoons pistachio nuts, split in half

sea salt and black pepper

1 Leave the saffron strands to soak in the chicken stock. Heat the oil in a large casserole or a small, heavy-bottomed roasting pan, add the onion and cook gently until softened.

2 Add the rice and chopped turkey and stir well to coat them with the oil. Add the saffron stock, orange juice, sugar and crushed cardamom seeds and season well with salt and pepper. Cover the mixture with a sheet of buttered wax paper, letting it rest on the surface. Transfer to an oven preheated to 325°F and bake for 25–35 minutes, until the rice is just tender, adding more stock if it dries out.

3 Remove the pilaf from the oven, fluff up the rice with a fork and sprinkle with the almonds and pistachio nuts.

PAELLA

Paella is a great dish to cook for a crowd. You will need a large pan, preferably a paella pan — otherwise a large frying pan will do.

Serves 8

1 small rabbit or chicken, cut into 10 pieces (you can ask your butcher to do this)

olive oil

1 teaspoon paprika

½ large Spanish onion, sliced

18 ounces ripe tomatoes, skinned, deseeded and chopped (see page 135)

½ red pepper, deseeded and chopped

2 garlic cloves, finely chopped

2 bay leaves

1 tablespoon chopped marjoram

1⅔ cups chicken stock (see pages 30–31)

a good pinch of saffron strands

3.5 ounces chorizo, sliced

1 large squid

1 pound sea bass fillet, skinned and cut into chunks

8 large raw shrimp

¾ cup white wine

18 ounces mussels, cleaned and de-bearded (see page 122)

7 ounces risotto rice or paella rice

1 jar of artichoke hearts, drained and cut in half

sea salt and black pepper

To garnish:

a handful of black olives

2½ tablespoons chopped parsley

1 lemon, cut in wedges

1 Season the rabbit or chicken pieces all over with salt and pepper. Heat about 3 1/2 tablespoons of olive oil in your paella pan or large frying pan over medium heat and fry the rabbit or chicken on all sides until brown. Add the paprika and onion and cook gently until the onion has softened. Now add the tomatoes, red pepper, garlic, bay leaves, marjoram, chicken stock, saffron and some salt and pepper and bring to a simmer. Reduce the heat and cook gently for 20 minutes.

2 Meanwhile, heat a little oil in another pan, add the chorizo and cook until browned all over. Remove from the pan and set aside. Clean the squid by pulling out and discarding the contents of the body sac and washing it thoroughly. Cut off the tentacles and slice the body into rings. Season the squid rings and tentacles, then brown them in the chorizo pan with a tablespoon of olive oil. Remove from the pan and set aside. Season the sea bass, cook it in the same pan until browned, then set aside with the squid and chorizo. Finally, cook the shrimp until they turn pink. Set them aside too.

3 Bring the wine to a boil in a large saucepan, add the mussels, then cover and steam over a high heat for 3–4 minutes, shaking the pan occasionally, until they open (discard any that remain closed). Take out the mussels with a slotted spoon, leave until cool enough to handle, then remove half of them from their shells. Strain the mussel cooking liquor through a fine sieve.

4 Add the rice and the strained mussel cooking liquor to the rabbit or chicken and tomatoes and continue cooking over a low heat for 15 minutes. Add the fish, chorizo, artichoke hearts and shelled mussels. Cover and cook for 15 minutes or until the rice is just tender. Season to taste.

5 Garnish the paella with the olives, unshelled mussels, chopped parsley and lemon wedges and serve straight from the pan.

MILD SPICED RICE PUDDING

I am one of those people who love the skin on a rice pudding – it's the best part. The spices add a soothing warmth to this simple dish.

Serves 4

2 tablespoons unsalted butter

1.5 ounces short grain rice

1.5 ounces superfine sugar

½ teaspoon freshly grated nutmeg

a pinch of ground cloves

2 strips of orange zest (removed from the orange with a potato peeler)

2½ cups whole milk (or half milk and half heavy cream)

1 Grease a 4-cup ovenproof dish with the butter and put the rice in it. Mix the sugar with the spices, sprinkle it over the rice and add the strips of orange zest.

2 Pour the milk over, then place in an oven preheated to 300°F. Bake for about 2 hours, stirring after the first half hour, until the rice is tender, the surface is golden brown and most of the milk has been absorbed.

COCONUT RICE PUDDING WITH RUM AND PINEAPPLE

Coconut and rice is an all-time classic, while the rum and pineapple elevate it to a luxury dish. This is cooked on the stovetop, making it much quicker than the traditional baked rice pudding.

Serves 4

1¼ cups coconut milk

4 ounces short grain rice

1 cup milk

1.5 ounces sugar, plus 2½ tablespoons for the pineapple

5 tablespoons heavy cream

2 tablespoons unsalted butter

½ ripe pineapple, peeled, cored and cut into cubes

2½ tablespoons rum

a few mint sprigs, to garnish (optional)

1 If using canned coconut milk, pour it into a bowl and stir well before using.

2 Put the rice, coconut milk and milk into a large, heavy-bottomed pan, bring to a simmer, then reduce the heat and cook gently for about 20 minutes, stirring frequently, until the rice is tender. Add the 1.5 ounces sugar and continue cooking for 10 minutes. Remove from the heat and leave to cool. Stir in the cream and then use the mixture to fill four 3-inch ramekins lined with plastic wrap. Smooth the tops and chill thoroughly.

3 Shortly before serving, heat the butter in a frying pan, add the pineapple and cook over a medium heat until beginning to color slightly. Remove and set aside. Add the 2 tablespoons of sugar and the rum and cook until the sugar has melted. Return the pineapple to the pan and stir to coat. Remove from the heat.

4 Turn out the rice on to each serving plate and top with the caramelized pineapple. Garnish with sprigs of mint, if you like, and serve.

PASTA

I often make fresh pasta but this chapter focuses
on the dried variety. It is so good nowadays that
there is no shame in using store-bought. However,
there are certain rules to be observed when
cooking dried pasta, and also when it comes to
saucing it. As with so many simple things, you
will be amply rewarded if you take the trouble to
do it well.

This is perhaps the most basic and familiar of all pasta dishes,
but if you've only ever made a pasta sauce with canned tomatoes
the flavors here will be a revelation. Make sure you use really
good, ripe tomatoes. This is bound to become a family favorite.

PASTA
with fresh tomato sauce

To skin and deseed tomatoes, follow steps 1 to 5
To cook pasta, follow steps 10 to 11

SERVES 4

14 ounces dried fusilli or other chunky pasta,
such as penne

5 tablespoons freshly grated Parmesan cheese

FOR THE TOMATO SAUCE:

2¼ pounds ripe but firm tomatoes

5 tablespoons olive oil

1 small onion, finely chopped

2 garlic cloves, finely chopped

1 teaspoon dried oregano

1 tablespoon tomato paste

1 teaspoon sugar

sea salt and black pepper

1 To skin and deseed the tomatoes, score a cross on the top of each one.

2 Put them in a pan of boiling water for 25 seconds.

3 Then transfer the tomatoes to a bowl of ice water.

4 Remove the tomatoes from the bowl and peel off the skin.

5 Cut each tomato into quarters, remove the seeds and roughly chop the flesh.

6 Heat the olive oil in a large, heavy-bottomed frying pan, add the onion and cook until soft but not colored.

7 Stir in the garlic, tomatoes and oregano.

8 Bring to a simmer and cook over a medium heat until the sauce starts to thicken.

9 Stir in the tomato paste and sugar, season with salt and pepper and cook for 2 minutes longer.

10 Put a large pan of water on to boil – you will need at least 12 cups of well-salted water. It is ready for the pasta when it reaches a rolling boil.

11 Add the pasta and cook until *al dente* – take out a piece and check a few minutes before the cooking time stated on the package is up.

12 When ready, drain well, season with salt and pepper and toss with the tomato sauce. Serve immediately, with the grated Parmesan.

tomato sauce variations

Pasta with Tomato and Ricotta Sauce – follow the recipe on pages 134–135 and crumble in 9 ounces ricotta cheese after tossing the pasta with the sauce. Serve with grated Parmesan.

Pasta with Tomato and Seared Fennel Sauce – cut 2 large fennel bulbs lengthwise down the center into 8 pieces each, keeping the root attached so the wedges don't fall to pieces. Sprinkle with oil and season well, then cook in a heavy-bottomed frying pan until very tender; this can take up to 20 minutes. Stir in half the Tomato Sauce from pages 134–135, season with salt and pepper, then cook for 2 minutes longer. Toss with the cooked pasta and serve sprinkled with 5 tablespoons grated Gruyère cheese. Orecchiette pasta works particularly well with this.

Pasta with Tomato and Basil Sauce – stir bunches of torn basil leaves into the Tomato Sauce from pages 134–135.

Pasta Amatriciana – cut 5 ounces pancetta into slices and fry in a little olive oil until crisp. Stir in a diced red pepper and cook until softened, then add a good pinch of chili powder and the Tomato and Basil Sauce (above) and cook for 10 minutes longer. Serve with spaghetti and grated pecorino.

Pasta with Tomato and Seafood Sauce – stir some steamed clams or mussels into the Tomato Sauce from pages 134–135.

TIPS AND IDEAS

■ A fresh tomato sauce will only taste as good as the tomatoes you use. Try to find a variety with plenty of flavor, and make sure they are ripe but quite firm.

■ If good fresh tomatoes aren't available, canned tomatoes make an excellent sauce too. Just remember to cook them for a little longer so the excess liquid evaporates.

■ When buying pasta, choose a good-quality Italian brand for the best results.

■ Dried egg ribbon pasta, such as tagliatelle, fettuccine and pappardelle, are more expensive than plain dried pasta but they are usually very good quality and take only 2 or 3 minutes to cook.

■ Never cram pasta into a small pan. The pan should be large enough to allow the pasta to move freely in the water as it cooks.

■ Pasta must never be overcooked; it should be slightly *al dente*, which means it still has a little resistance when you bite it.

■ Hold back a little of the pasta cooking water and use it to adjust the consistency of the sauce if necessary, once it is coating the pasta.

■ Pasta should be tossed with the sauce, rather like dressing a salad. There is nothing worse than naked pasta with a blob of sauce on top. The role of the sauce is to flavor and lubricate the pasta.

■ Leftover sauced pasta can be used to make a frittata (see page 76).

PASTA WITH UNCOOKED TOMATO SAUCE

This is served at room temperature, making it a delicious summer pasta dish. You could add diced zucchini or cucumber. The trick is to make sure that everything is very finely chopped.

Serves 4

2¼ pounds ripe tomatoes, skinned and deseeded (see page 135), then cut into very fine dice

1 garlic clove, crushed

1 shallot, very finely chopped

¼ cup white wine vinegar

⅔ cup best-quality extra virgin olive oil

14 ounces conchiglie (pasta shells)

fine sea salt and black pepper

1 Put the diced tomatoes in a bowl and stir in the garlic and shallot. Season with salt and pepper, then add the vinegar and olive oil.

2 Cook the pasta in a large pan of boiling salted water according to the instructions on page 135. When it is *al dente*, drain well, toss with the sauce and adjust the seasoning. Leave to cool to room temperature before serving.

FETTUCCINE WITH PESTO

I have given the traditional method of making pesto using a pestle and mortar but if you want a smoother mixture, you can make it in a food processor instead.

Serves 4

3.5 ounces basil leaves

1 teaspoon coarse sea salt

1 garlic clove, finely chopped

1 ounce pine nuts

2 ounces Parmesan cheese, freshly grated, plus 2 ounces extra to serve

⅔ cup olive oil

11 ounces dried egg fettuccine

sea salt and black pepper

1 First make the pesto. Put some of the basil leaves in a mortar with the salt and crush them with the pestle. Gradually add the remaining basil leaves, working them with the pestle, then add the garlic and pound until well incorporated. Add the pine nuts and pound to a rough paste. Mix in the Parmesan and then gradually mix in the olive oil. Season to taste.

2 Cook the fettuccine in a large pan of boiling salted water according to the instructions on page 135. When it is *al dente*, drain well, toss with the pesto immediately and adjust the seasoning. Serve with the extra Parmesan.

pesto variations

Basil and Walnut Pesto – follow the recipe above, replacing half the pine nuts with walnuts.

Sun-dried Tomato Pesto – replace the basil in the recipe above with a 9-ounce jar of sun-dried tomatoes in olive oil, drained. Whiz all the ingredients together in a food processor and season to taste.

FETTUCCINE WITH CARROTS AND ZUCCHINI

I came up with this dish when I had a glut of zucchini in the summer, and sat outside eating it with my assistant, Belinda. It made a truly memorable meal.

Serves 4

18 ounces slender new-season carrots

2 medium zucchini (it looks attractive if you use 1 yellow summer squash and 1 green zucchini)

6 tablespoons unsalted butter

1 garlic clove, finely chopped

2½ tablespoons all-purpose flour

1 cup whole milk

3.5 ounces Cheddar cheese, grated

7 tablespoons finely chopped parsley

5 tablespoons chopped tarragon (optional)

11 ounces dried egg fettuccine

sea salt and black pepper

1 Slice the carrots very finely. This can be done on a mandoline, if you have one. Cut the zucchini in half lengthwise, then slice finely across. Melt the butter in a heavy-bottomed frying pan, add the carrots and cook over a very low heat for about 5 minutes, until just tender. Remove and set aside. Add the zucchini and garlic to the pan and cook for 5 minutes longer, then set aside with the carrots.

2 Sprinkle the flour into the pan and cook for 1 minute, stirring gently. Gradually stir in the milk and bring to a simmer. When the sauce thickens, stir in the Cheddar cheese, parsley and tarragon, if using, and season well with salt and pepper. Return the carrots and zucchini to the pan.

3 Cook the fettuccine in a large pan of boiling salted water according to the instructions on page 135. When it is *al dente*, drain well and toss with the sauce. Adjust the seasoning and serve.

LASAGNE WITH BOLOGNESE SAUCE

Serves 4

2½ tablespoons olive oil

1 large onion, very finely chopped

2 celery stalks, finely chopped

2 garlic cloves, finely chopped

1¼ pounds ground beef

¾ cup red wine

4 tomatoes, skinned, deseeded and chopped (see page 135)

14-ounce can of chopped tomatoes

1 teaspoon dried oregano

2 bay leaves

2 tablespoons tomato paste

1 teaspoon sugar

2 quantities of Béchamel Sauce (see pages 44–45)

11 ounces fresh pasta sheets

2 ounces Parmesan cheese, freshly grated

sea salt and black pepper

1 Heat the oil in a large, heavy-bottomed saucepan, add the onion, celery and garlic and cook until soft but not browned. Turn the heat up, stir in the minced beef and separate the strands in the pan with a fork. Pour in the red wine and simmer for 2 minutes. Turn the heat down and stir in the fresh and canned tomatoes, oregano and bay leaves. Cover the pan and simmer over a low heat for 40 minutes. Remove the lid and continue to cook for 20 minutes, until the mixture is reduced and thickened. Stir in the tomato paste and sugar and season with salt and pepper.

2 If necessary, gently reheat the béchamel sauce. Spread a couple of tablespoons of the Bolognese sauce over the base of a large, rectangular ovenproof dish, and cover with a layer of pasta sheets. Spoon on a layer of béchamel, then repeat this process until all the ingredients are used up, finishing with a layer of béchamel. Sprinkle with the Parmesan and place in an oven preheated to 350°F. Bake for 45 minutes, until browned and bubbling.

ORECCHIETTE WITH GORGONZOLA, SPINACH AND ROASTED RED PEPPER SAUCE

Serves 4

4 red peppers

olive oil

½ small onion, finely chopped

2 garlic cloves, finely chopped

2 tablespoons unsalted butter

11 ounces fresh spinach, washed, stems removed

14 ounces orecchiette pasta

4 ounces gorgonzola cheese, crumbled

2 ounces pecorino cheese, grated

sea salt and black pepper

1 Put the red peppers in a roasting pan and drizzle a little oil over them. Place in an oven preheated to 375°F and roast for 20 minutes, until patched with brown, turning halfway through. Cool a little and then peel off the skin. Remove the seeds and roughly chop the flesh.

2 Drizzle some oil into a large frying pan, add the onion and cook gently until softened. Add the garlic and red pepper and season well with salt and pepper. Put into a blender or food processor and whiz to a purée, then transfer to a saucepan and set aside.

3 Melt the butter in a saucepan, add the spinach and cook briefly over a medium heat until wilted. Drain well, season and set aside.

4 Cook the orecchiette in a large pan of boiling salted water until *al dente*, then drain well. Thoroughly heat the red pepper sauce and toss with the drained pasta, then fold in the gorgonzola, pecorino and wilted spinach. Adjust the seasoning and serve.

SPAGHETTI CARBONARA

This is a very quick pasta dish if you are stuck for time. I love lots of black pepper with it.

Serves 4

14 ounces spaghetti

olive oil

7 ounces pancetta or bacon, diced

1 garlic clove, finely chopped

2 large eggs

3.5 ounces pecorino cheese, freshly grated

3.5 ounces Parmesan cheese, freshly grated

2½ teaspoons black pepper

sea salt

1 Cook the spaghetti in a large pan of boiling salted water, according to the instructions on page 135. Meanwhile, drizzle some olive oil into a large frying pan, add the pancetta and fry until crisp, but don't let it get too dark. Add the garlic and mix well, then remove from the heat.

2 Whisk the eggs in a bowl with 2.5 ounces each of the pecorino and Parmesan, then season with the black pepper and some salt.

3 When the pasta is *al dente*, drain, reserving a little of the cooking water. Add the spaghetti to the pancetta in the frying pan and heat until very hot. Stir in 3 1/2 tablespoons of the reserved cooking water, then remove from the heat and fold in the egg mixture; the eggs will cook in the heat of the pasta. Toss very well, adjust the seasoning, then serve, accompanied by the remaining cheese. I always put more black pepper on top.

TAGLIATELLE WITH SEAFOOD SAUCE

The trick here is to be careful not to overcook the seafood, otherwise it will be rubbery. You can prepare the fish in advance, however, and just reheat it quickly at the last minute — making life so much easier if you have people coming for dinner.

Serves 4

9 ounces raw shrimp in their shells

1⅔ cups fish stock (see page 35)

7 ounces clams

¾ cup white wine

olive oil

½ red chile, very finely chopped

2 garlic cloves, very finely chopped

7 ounces cleaned small squid bodies, cut into rounds about ⅛ inch thick

¾ cup heavy cream

14 ounces tagliatelle

1 tablespoon finely chopped chives

sea salt and black pepper

1 Shell the shrimp and put the shells into a saucepan with the fish stock. Boil until the stock has reduced by half, then strain through a fine sieve and set aside. Slice the shrimp horizontally in half, dry them well and set aside.

2 Scrub the clams clean under cold running water, discarding any with open shells that don't close when tapped lightly on a work surface. Put the white wine in a large saucepan and bring to a boil. Add the clams, cover the pan with a lid and steam over high heat for 3–4 minutes, shaking the pan occasionally, until they open. Remove the clams from the saucepan, discarding any that have refused to open, and strain the cooking juices through a fine sieve into a bowl.

3 Drizzle some olive oil into a large frying pan, add the shrimp and sear briefly on both sides over fairly high heat. Add the chile and garlic and toss well. Remove the mixture from the pan and set aside. Now add the squid rings to the frying pan and cook over high heat for 1 minute, no more – if you overcook squid, it will become tough and chewy. Add to the shrimp. Finally pour the clam cooking juices into the pan and bring to a boil, stirring and scraping the base of the pan with a wooden spoon to deglaze it. Pour in the reduced fish stock and simmer for 4 minutes, then add the cream and cook for 2 minutes, until slightly thickened. Season well. Return all the seafood to the pan and heat through gently. Stir in the chives.

4 Cook the tagliatelle in a large pan of boiling salted water until *al dente*, then drain. Toss with the sauce, adjust the seasoning and serve.

GRILLING
and
FRYING

Griddle pans have become very popular over the last few years, blurring the distinction between grilling and frying. A ridged grill pan is fun to use, as you can make neat char lines on the food. It's also practical because the fat runs down between the ridges, leaving the meat or fish nice and dry. If you don't have a ridged grill pan, you can use a decent, heavy-bottomed frying pan for pretty much anything.

The timings in this recipe will give medium-rare steak; cook slightly less or more, depending on your preference and on the thickness of the steak. Steak really does taste better when served rare. It is more tender and more flavorful. If you think you don't like it, give it another try — when it is cooked correctly, it tastes wonderful.

SIRLOIN STEAK

with *Béarnaise sauce*

SERVES 4

4 thick sirloin steaks (about ¾ inch thick), weighing about 6 ounces each

olive oil

a knob of butter

sea salt and black pepper

TO SERVE:

1 quantity of Béarnaise Sauce (see page 60)

Potato Wedges (see page 199)

1 Take your steaks out of the fridge and allow them to come to room temperature. Rub with a little olive oil and season well on both sides.

2 Heat a ridged griddle pan over medium-high heat until it is very hot, then drizzle in a little olive oil.

3 Place the steaks on the pan and turn down the heat slightly. Cook them for 2 minutes without moving, otherwise you will spoil the griddle markings.

4 Turn them through 90 degrees so you get criss-cross markings underneath – if the steaks stick when you try to move them, leave them for a minute longer.

5 Cook for 2 minutes again, then turn over and repeat on the other side.

6 To test if the steak is done, you can use a meat thermometer: it should register 115°F for rare, 130°F for medium or 150–160°F for well done.

7 Alternatively, just press the meat with your finger: the more it is cooked, the tighter and firmer it becomes. If you can push it down a little, it is cooked rare.

8 Swirl the knob of butter into the griddle pan.

9 Then remove the steaks and leave on a plate to rest for 5 minutes. Serve with the Béarnaise Sauce and Potato Wedges.

TIPS AND IDEAS

■ Make sure the meat is at room temperature before cooking. This relaxes it and makes it easier to judge the cooking time.

■ If you don't have a ridged griddle pan, just cook the steaks in a good, heavy-bottomed frying pan.

■ If you are cooking more than one steak at a time, make sure they are not too close together or they will steam rather than fry.

■ Resting the steak after cooking is crucial, as it tenderizes it and completes the cooking process. As the meat relaxes, most of the juices are absorbed back into it, creating a succulent texture.

sirloin steak variations

Sirloin Steak with Chile and Garlic
– pound some finely chopped garlic and
fresh chile with a little olive oil to make a
paste. Rub the paste over the steaks and
then cook as on pages 148–149.

**Sirloin Steak with Mushroom
Sauce** – cook the steaks in a plain
frying pan rather than a ridged griddle
pan. While they are resting, pour
5 tablespoons of brandy into the pan
and bring to a boil, stirring and scraping
the base of the pan with a wooden
spoon to deglaze it. When the brandy
has reduced by half, pour it through a
fine sieve into a bowl. Wipe the pan
clean, add 4 tablespoons unsalted butter
and cook 9 ounces sliced mushrooms in
it until softened. Continue to cook till all
the liquid has been absorbed back into
the mushrooms, then add ½ cup heavy
cream. Bring to a simmer, pour in the
brandy and season well. Serve with the
steaks.

**Sirloin Steak with Pink or Green
Peppercorn Sauce** – cook the steaks
in a plain frying pan rather than a ridged
griddle pan. While they are resting, pour
5 tablespoons of red wine into the pan
and bring to a boil, stirring and scraping
the bottom of the pan with a wooden
spoon to deglaze it. When the wine has
reduced by half, pour it through a fine
sieve into a bowl. Wipe the pan clean,
add 4 tablespoons unsalted butter to it,
then add 1 tablespoon of drained pink
or green peppercorns in vinegar. Cook
for 1 minute, pour in ¾ cup heavy cream
and simmer until slightly thickened. Stir
in the red wine, season well, then serve
with the steaks.

GENERAL FRYING AND GRILLING PRINCIPLES

■ Season the food on both sides with salt and pepper
before you put it in the pan, and then again when it is
cooked. You will be surprised how much seasoning it
can take.

■ Place the pan over a high heat until thoroughly hot
and then turn it down as soon as you add the food. This
will prevent the outside from getting too dark before the
middle is done.

■ I like to use olive oil for frying and grilling. When I fry,
I tend to finish it off by adding a little butter, which gives
richness and color.

■ Don't overcrowd the pan, or the temperature will drop
too much when you put the food in, causing it to steam
rather than fry.

■ Once the food is in the pan, don't touch it for at least
a minute or two, to allow a crust to form underneath.
Depending on the thickness of your piece of meat or fish,
you may need to leave it for a little more or less time.

■ If your piece of meat or fish is particularly thick, you
can complete the cooking by transferring it to a moderate
oven for 3–4 minutes.

■ Meat should always be allowed to rest after frying or
grilling. I generally allow it to rest for half the amount of
time it took to cook.

■ When cooking fish, I always fry or grill it skin-side
down first. Make several slashes in the skin before
cooking, to help keep it flat and enable it to cook through.

■ Once the fish is in the pan, leave well enough alone;
if you try to move it before it is ready to be turned, it can
stick and tear. Dusting thin-skinned fish with a little flour
before cooking can help prevent this.

■ If you have a lot of people coming to dinner, you can
brown your meat on both sides (just the skin side for fish)
in advance, then put it on a baking tray. Finish it off in a
moderately high oven when your guests arrive.

LAMB CHOPS WITH FENNEL, PEAS AND MINT

Serves 4

a little olive oil

8 lamb chops

4 tablespoons unsalted butter

sea salt and black pepper

crab apple jelly or mint jelly, to serve

For the vegetables:

2 fennel bulbs

3 tablespoons unsalted butter

a drizzle of olive oil

2 sprigs of thyme

¼ cup chicken stock (see pages 30–31)

½ cup heavy cream

11 ounces frozen petite peas, defrosted

1 rounded tablespoon chopped mint, plus extra to serve

1 Cut each fennel bulb lengthways in half, then slice each half into 6. Heat the butter and oil in a heavy-bottomed frying pan, add the fennel and thyme and cook, turning occasionally, until the fennel has softened but not browned. Add the stock and toss well. Pour in the cream and simmer for a few minutes, until it starts to thicken. Stir in the peas and season to taste.

2 Rub a little olive oil over the lamb chops and season well on both sides with salt and pepper. Heat a heavy-bottomed frying pan over medium heat, drizzle in a little olive oil, then lay the chops in the pan. Turn the heat down a little so they do not burn. Cook for 3 minutes without moving them. Now turn onto the other side and continue cooking for 3 minutes. Add the butter and baste the chops with it as it melts. Cook for another minute, then remove the chops from the pan to a warm plate and leave to rest for 4 minutes.

3 Stir the mint into the fennel and peas. Divide the mixture between 4 serving plates, put the lamb chops on top and sprinkle with mint. Serve with a small bowl of crab apple jelly or mint jelly on the side.

DUCK BREASTS WITH BLACKCURRANT SAUCE

Blackcurrants are a lovely strong, acidic fruit, making them an ideal accompaniment to duck or game.

Serves 4

4 duck breasts

olive oil

sea salt and black pepper

For the blackcurrant sauce:

2 tablespoons unsalted butter

2 shallots, finely chopped

½ cup red wine

1 tablespoon blackcurrant (or redcurrant) jelly

14 ounces fresh or frozen blackcurrants

½ cup chicken stock (see pages 30–31)

1 Score the skin of each duck breast with a sharp knife about 5 times, then season with salt and pepper. Get a large, dry heavy-bottomed frying pan smoking hot. Put in the duck skin-side down, turn the heat down to medium and leave for about 5 minutes. Turn over and cook for 3 minutes. Remove from the heat and leave to rest for at least 5 minutes. This will give quite pink meat. If you want to cook the duck a little more, put it in the oven at 375°F for 2–3 minutes before resting.

2 To make the sauce, melt the butter in a non-stick saucepan, add the shallots and cook gently until very soft. Add the red wine, bring to a boil and cook for 30 seconds. Add the jelly and blackcurrants, mix well, then add the stock. Bring to a boil and cook for 1 minute. Transfer to a blender and whiz to a purée, then strain through a sieve. Reheat gently and season to taste.

3 Slice the duck breasts into 3–5 pieces and put them on a cloth to absorb the juices. Serve with a little of the sauce poured over and the rest on the plate, accompanied by Braised Red Cabbage with Pears (see page 202).

MACKEREL WITH CANNELLINI BEANS

You can broil or fry the mackerel here but I prefer it fried, as it gives a richer flavor. Thin-skinned fish are always easier to cook if you dredge them with flour first to make them crisper. I never soak dried beans, I just cook them for longer. But of course, you can soak them in cold water overnight before cooking if you prefer.

Serves 4

4 mackerel, cleaned

olive oil and 2½ tablespoons all-purpose flour, if frying

3½ tablespoons unsalted butter

sea salt and black pepper

For the cannellini beans:

7 ounces dried cannellini beans

1 onion, cut into quarters

extra virgin olive oil

2 bacon slices, finely chopped

2 garlic cloves, finely chopped

5 tablespoons chopped parsley

1 Rinse the cannellini beans in a sieve, then put them in a large saucepan with the onion, cover generously with water and bring to a boil. Reduce the heat and simmer for 1 1/2–2 hours, until tender. Drain well and set aside.

2 Heat a little olive oil in a frying pan, add the chopped bacon and fry until crisp. Stir in the garlic, then toss in the beans with the parsley. Remove from the heat, season to taste with salt and pepper and add 2 1/2 tablespoons of extra virgin olive oil.

3 Season the mackerel with salt. If you are frying it, season the flour well with salt and pepper and dredge the fish in it. Heat a large, ovenproof frying pan, drizzle in some oil and then add the butter. Fry the mackerel over medium heat for 2 minutes, until golden brown underneath, then turn over the fish and transfer the pan to an oven preheated to 375°F. Cook for 6 minutes, until the fish is done.

4 To broil the mackerel, melt the butter, brush the fish all over with it and season well inside the fish. Put the mackerel under a broiler preheated to medium and cook for 4 minutes, until golden brown. Turn and broil for another 4 minutes, basting occasionally, until cooked through.

5 Serve the mackerel on top of the cannellini beans.

GRIDDLED SPICY CHICKEN

Chicken can take on lots of gorgeous flavors and this recipe is no exception. It works very well on a barbecue.

Serves 4

4 large, skinless chicken breasts

olive oil for drizzling

sea salt and black pepper

For the marinade:

4 ounces plain yogurt

⅛ cup olive oil

2½ teaspoons ground cumin

2½ teaspoons ground coriander

2½ teaspoons hot curry powder

1 garlic clove, finely chopped

1 Put all the marinade ingredients in a bowl and mix well. Add the chicken breasts, make sure they are well coated in the marinade and season well with salt and pepper. Cover with plastic wrap and refrigerate for at least 30 minutes.

2 Heat a ridged griddle pan and drizzle with olive oil. Lay the chicken breasts on it and cook over a medium heat for about 5 minutes on each side, until cooked through. Remove from the griddle and leave to rest for 5 minutes. Serve with a green salad (see pages 12–13) and Rice Pilaf (see page 127).

PORK CHOPS WITH SPINACH AND MADEIRA SAUCE

Serves 4

4 pork chops

2½ tablespoons olive oil

1 tablespoon unsalted butter

sea salt and black pepper

For the Madeira sauce:

1 shallot, finely chopped

1 garlic clove, finely chopped

⅔ cup Madeira

1 cup chicken stock (see pages 30–31)

½ cup heavy cream

For the spinach:

5 tablespoons unsalted butter

2 pounds fresh spinach, large stems removed

grated nutmeg

1 Season the pork chops on both sides. Place a large, heavy-bottomed frying pan over a high heat and, when it is hot, drizzle in the oil. Add the chops, reduce the heat to medium and fry for 4–5 minutes on each side, just until firm. They should not be overcooked. Add the butter to the pan and baste the chops with it as it melts. Transfer the chops to a dish and leave to rest for 5 minutes.

2 Meanwhile, make the sauce. Add the shallot and garlic to the frying pan and cook, stirring, for 2 minutes, until softened. Add the Madeira and boil until reduced by half. Pour in the chicken stock and cream, bring back to a boil and simmer until reduced and slightly thickened. Season to taste with salt and pepper and strain through a fine sieve.

3 For the spinach, melt 3 1/2 tablespoons of the butter in a large saucepan, add the spinach and cook over a low heat until wilted. Drain very thoroughly, then put it back into the pan, add the rest of the butter and season with salt, pepper and a good pinch of nutmeg. Serve the chops on the spinach, surrounded by the sauce.

BROILED COD WITH BRAISED LEEKS AND HOLLANDAISE SAUCE

Cod needs to have succulent, milky flakes, so be very careful not to overcook it.

Serves 4

4 pieces of cod fillet, weighing 6 ounces each

olive oil

1 quantity of Hollandaise Sauce (see pages 56–58)

sea salt and black pepper

chopped chives, to garnish

For the braised leeks:

4 leeks

4 tablespoons unsalted butter, melted

½ cup chicken stock (see pages 30–31)

1 Trim the leeks by slitting them open lengthways and rinsing all the dirt out, then discarding the outer layers and cutting off the root. Cut into 2-inch lengths. Grease a gratin dish with a little of the melted butter, arrange the leeks in it in neat rows, then pour over the rest of the butter, followed by the stock. Season well with salt and pepper, cover and place in an oven preheated to 375°F. Bake for 40 minutes, until the leeks are soft.

2 Brush the cod all over with olive oil and season well with salt and plenty of black pepper. Place in a baking pan and broil, skin-side up, under a medium heat for 5 minutes. Transfer to the oven and cook for 2 minutes or until the fish is cooked through. If the fillet is quite thin, you will only need to broil it for 3 minutes and finish off in the oven for 2 minutes.

3 Leave the cod to rest for 5 minutes. Drain the leeks well, then serve the cod on top of the leeks, accompanied by the hollandaise sauce and garnished with chopped chives.

SEARED SALMON WITH CHILE AND LIME

I like a nice, golden crust on this fish, but remember that salmon always needs to be slightly undercooked rather than overcooked, otherwise it can be dry.

Serves 4

26 ounces middle-cut salmon fillet, skin on, cut into 4 slices

juice of 2 limes

2 tablespoons peanut oil

For the marinade:

1 shallot, chopped

2 garlic cloves, chopped

⅓ cup extra virgin olive oil

1 teaspoon ground coriander

¾-inch piece of fresh ginger, chopped

2 bird's eye chiles, chopped

sea salt and black pepper

1 Put all the marinade ingredients into a food processor and whiz to a purée. Put the salmon into a bowl, cover with the marinade and leave for a couple of hours. Just before cooking the salmon, wipe off the marinade and sprinkle on the lime juice.

2 Heat the peanut oil in a large, non-stick frying pan, add the fish, skin-side down, and cook over medium heat for 4–6 minutes. Turn it over and cook for 2–3 minutes longer, depending on the thickness of the fish – it should be slightly underdone in the middle. Remove and leave to rest for 5 minutes, then serve. It is very good with bok choy.

ROASTS

The problem with roasts very often is knowing exactly how long to cook them. With experience, you will learn to judge by look and feel, but in the meantime this chapter suggests some basic principles to follow. A little bit of patience and understanding — and a really good piece of meat with enough fat to keep it tender and moist — will give you the perfect roast.

This is a simple dish to prepare and makes a perfect family meal, but it will only be as good as the chicken you buy. I always choose free-range or organic birds, because they have so much flavor. They cost more than factory-farmed chickens, so make sure you use every scrap of meat. Even the carcass can be used to make stock for soup (see Tips and Ideas, page 32).

ROAST CHICKEN

SERVES 4

1 free-range or organic chicken, weighing about 4 pounds

6 sprigs of thyme

1 lemon, sliced into 8

4 tablespoons softened unsalted butter

1 onion, roughly chopped

1 carrot, roughly chopped

1 leek, roughly chopped

sea salt and black pepper

FOR THE GRAVY:

1 teaspoon all-purpose flour

¾ cup white wine

1½ cups chicken stock (see pages 30–31)

1 Take the chicken out of the fridge a good hour before cooking. Remove any string from the bird and take the bag of giblets, if there is one, out of the cavity.

2 Season inside the cavity with salt and pepper and then put the thyme sprigs and half the lemon slices inside the cavity.

3 Smear the butter all over the bird and season with salt and pepper.

4 Put the vegetables and the remaining lemon slices into a heavy-bottomed roasting pan in which the chicken will just fit.

5 Season with salt and pepper and put the chicken on top breast-side down, so the juices will fall through the vegetables as it cooks.

6 Place the chicken in an oven preheated to 400°F and roast for 30 minutes.

7 Turn the chicken over and sprinkle some sea salt over it. Reduce the oven temperature to 350°F, and return the pan to the oven.

8 Roast for another 45 minutes, basting the bird once or twice with the fat in the roasting pan.

9 To test the chicken for doneness, take hold of a leg and it should wobble.

10 You can also insert a knife in the thickest part of the thigh, near the bone – if the juices run clear the chicken is done.

11 Put the chicken onto a warmed platter and leave to rest for at least 15 minutes while you make the gravy.

12 Discard the vegetables from the pan and pour off most of the fat, leaving the chicken residue behind.

13 Put the roasting pan on the stovetop over a low heat, sprinkle in the flour and mix well.

14 Pour in the white wine.

15 Bring to a simmer, stirring and scraping the base of the pan with a wooden spoon to deglaze it.

16 When the wine has reduced in volume by about half, gradually stir in the chicken stock and bring back to a boil.

17 Simmer until the gravy has reduced enough to give a good flavor – taste it to check.

18 Season to taste and strain into a small glass. Serve straight away, with the roast chicken. Gratin Dauphinois (see pages 192–193) makes a delicious accompaniment.

TIPS AND IDEAS

■ Seasoning the meat with coarse sea salt gives a good flavor and a crisp skin.

■ I like a lot of flavor in my roast chicken – hence the herbs and lemon in the cavity. You could also sit the chicken on big bunches of herbs such as rosemary and thyme, or on chopped leeks.

■ You don't have to put vegetables underneath the bird before roasting but they help keep it moist and add a delicious flavor to the juices, which are then used to make the gravy.

■ Start large roasts, such as a chicken or a piece of beef, at a high heat to give a good color, then turn the temperature down to allow the meat to cook through.

■ Basting occasionally with the fat in the roasting pan is important to give a good flavor and color.

■ Resting the chicken in a warm place on a warm serving platter for at least 15 minutes allows the bird to relax, making it easier to carve. This is a great opportunity to finish off the vegetables and gravy. When the meat has rested, you can tip off the juices that have collected in the plate and add them to your gravy or sauce.

■ A good roast needs fat to keep it moist during cooking, when it will break down and add flavor and succulence. When buying joints such as beef, look for a piece with nice creamy fat rather than white fat, which is a sign of intensive farming. Creamy fat is an indication that an animal has had a good life – and that it will taste better.

■ If your roast doesn't have any fat, you can add some – in the form of bacon for birds such as partridge, pigeon and guinea fowl, or a coating of oil on a joint of beef.

roast chicken variations

Chicken Roasted with Herb Butter
– put 5 ounces soft unsalted butter in a food processor, add 2 garlic cloves, 5 tablespoons of parsley and 2½ tablespoons each of cilantro, chives and thyme. Process to a purée and season well. Rub the herb butter all over and under the skin of the chicken, then roast as on pages 158–160.

Chicken Roasted with Curry Paste
– put in a food processor 1 chopped onion, a ¾-inch piece of fresh ginger, chopped, 1 chopped chile, 4 garlic cloves, 2½ teaspoons each of ground cumin, coriander, garam masala and turmeric, ¾ cup olive or vegetable oil, 2½ teaspoons of sugar and some salt and pepper. Whiz to a smooth purée, then rub all over the chicken, including the cavity, and leave to marinate for 1 hour. Put the chicken breast-side up in a roasting pan and roast at 350°F for 1½ hours. If the chicken darkens too quickly, cover loosely with foil. Transfer the bird to a board to rest, pour off excess fat from the pan, then stir in 6 ounces crème fraîche, a squeeze of lemon juice and some salt and pepper. Heat gently on the stovetop, stirring to deglaze the pan. Serve the chicken with the cream sauce and Rice Pilaf (see page 127).

ROAST BEEF

Serve with Yorkshire Pudding (see page 91), Roast Potatoes (see page 198) and spring greens.

Serves 6–8

one ribeye roast, weighing 5½–6 pounds

olive oil

1 large onion, sliced

1 large carrot, sliced

2 garlic cloves, chopped

4 sprigs of thyme

sea salt and black pepper

For the gravy:

⅔ cup red wine

2 cups beef stock (see page 34)

1 Season the beef all over with salt and pepper. Heat a heavy-bottomed roasting pan on the stovetop, add a drizzle of oil and brown the beef in it on all sides. Remove from the heat and throw in the onion, carrot, garlic and thyme. Make sure the beef is fat-side up in the pan, then put it into an oven preheated to 425°F and roast for 15 minutes. Turn the oven down to 325°F and roast for about an hour longer: I allow 15 minutes per pound plus an extra 15 minutes in total, for rare beef; if you want it more cooked, give it 20 minutes per pound.

2 When the beef is done to your liking, remove it from the oven and transfer to a warm platter. Cover loosely with foil and leave in a warm place to rest while you make the gravy.

3 Remove excess fat from the roasting pan. Add the red wine to the vegetables in the pan and bring to a boil, stirring and scraping the bottom of the pan. Boil for 2–3 minutes, then pour in the stock, bring back to a boil and simmer until reduced by half, so the flavor intensifies. Season well with salt and pepper and pour through a sieve into a clean pan. Reheat gently when ready to serve.

4 To carve the beef, cut the meat off the bone, then carve down.

ROAST LEG OF LAMB WITH ROSEMARY

I love to roast lamb on loads of rosemary to gain the flavor in the sauce.
This is delicious served with Cauliflower Cheese (see page 49).

Serves 6

1 leg of lamb on the bone, weighing about
5½ pounds (ask your butcher to remove the
pelvic bone, as this will make it easier to
carve)

8 sprigs of rosemary

5 garlic cloves, peeled and cut into thin slivers

1 large onion, sliced

olive oil

2 tablespoons redcurrant jelly

sea salt and black pepper

For the sauce:

¾ cup red wine

⅔ cup Marsala (optional)

2½ tablespoons redcurrant jelly

2½ tablespoons tomato paste

a sprig of rosemary

2 cups chicken stock (see pages 30–31)

Beurre Manié (see Tips and Ideas, page 48),
made with 0.35 ounces butter and
0.35 ounces flour

1 Make small slits in the skin of the lamb deep enough to hold the rosemary and garlic. Divide 2 of the rosemary sprigs into tiny sprigs and push a garlic sliver and a sprig of rosemary into each slit in the lamb. Season well with salt and pepper.

2 Put the sliced onion, the remaining sprigs of rosemary and the rest of the garlic in a large roasting pan and set aside. Heat a large frying pan, drizzle in some olive oil, then add the lamb and brown it all over. Place the lamb in the roasting pan and put it into an oven preheated to 400°F. Roast for about 1 1/2 hours: I allow 15 minutes per pound, plus an extra 15 minutes in total, to give pink meat; if you prefer it more cooked, give it 20 minutes per pound. Baste the meat a couple of times, and about halfway through the cooking, after the second basting, brush the redcurrant jelly all over it.

3 Once the lamb is done to your liking, remove it from the oven, place on a warm platter and leave to rest in a warm place for at least 15 minutes.

4 While the meat is resting, put the roasting pan on the stovetop and spoon off the excess fat. Add the red wine and the Marsala, if using, stirring well with a wooden spoon to take up all the lovely juices and caramelized bits from the base of the tin. Stir in the redcurrant jelly, then bring to a boil and simmer until the sauce starts to thicken. Add the tomato paste, the sprig of rosemary and chicken stock and bring back to a boil. Simmer until reduced and slightly thickened. Whisk the *beurre manié* into the sauce a small lump at a time to thicken it – you may not need it all. Simmer until the sauce thickens, then strain through a fine sieve into a clean saucepan; reheat gently and season to taste with salt and pepper. Carve the lamb and serve with the sauce.

SLOW-ROAST PORK BELLY WITH CHEESY MUSTARD SAUCE

Pork belly is an underrated piece of meat but I think it is one of the most delicious cuts of all. It is on the fatty side but so flavorful.

Serves 4

4½ pound piece of pork belly, skin finely scored (you can ask your butcher to do this or do it yourself with a utility knife)

4 garlic cloves, finely chopped

2½ teaspoons sea salt

1 large onion, finely sliced

4 large sprigs of thyme

olive oil

¾ cup chicken stock (see pages 30–31)

For the cheesy mustard sauce:

½ quantity of Béchamel Sauce (see pages 44–45)

2½ tablespoons Dijon mustard

2 ounces Cheddar cheese, grated

5 tablespoons heavy cream

2½ tablespoons dry vermouth (optional)

sea salt and white pepper

1 First cut the skin off the pork, trying to keep it in one piece and leaving the fat on the meat. Remove excess fat from under the belly. Rub the belly all over with the finely chopped garlic and half the salt, then rub the other half of the salt into the skin, making sure you get into those cuts. Put the skin back on top of the pork.

2 Put the sliced onion into a roasting pan and top with the thyme, then lay the pork belly on top. Sprinkle with a little olive oil and pour the chicken stock into the pan. Place in an oven preheated to 300°F and cook for 1 1/2 hours. Turn the oven up to 375°F and cook for 1 hour; it is ready when a knife inserted in the meat comes out without any resistance. Remove the pork from the oven, transfer it to a warm serving platter and leave to rest for 20 minutes. If the skin hasn't formed crackling, lift it off the pork, put it on a baking tray and return it to the oven for 15 minutes or so.

3 Reheat the béchamel sauce, if necessary. Stir in the mustard, cheese, cream and vermouth, if using, and cook very gently for 4 minutes. Adjust the seasoning.

4 Carve the pork into strips and serve with the sauce. You can simply break up the crackling to serve.

ROAST DUCK WITH HONEY AND SOY SAUCE

This is one of my favorite ways of eating duck. I love the crispy skin, very well cooked and with all the fat extracted. Serve with Roast Squash (page 196).

Serves 2–4

1 duck, weighing about 5½ pounds

sea salt and black pepper

For the honey and soy sauce:

3½ tablespoons runny honey

1 tablespoon red wine vinegar

5 tablespoons red wine

5 tablespoons soy sauce

1⅔ cups chicken stock (see pages 30–31)

3½ tablespoons cold unsalted butter, diced

1 Remove the white fat from inside the duck and the giblets too, if they have been supplied (you can use the giblets to make a simple stock, if you like). Now remove the wishbone: cut round the bone with a very sharp knife to release it from the flesh and then pull it off – this makes the duck easier to carve. Prick the skin covering the breast, being careful not to go through the flesh. Place the duck on a rack in a roasting pan, breast side up. Season with salt and pepper and put into an oven preheated to 350°F. Roast for 25 minutes, then turn the duck over onto its breast and cook for another 25 minutes. Now turn it back the right way up and cook for 50 minutes until the skin is very brown and crisp. Remove from the pan and allow to rest for 15 minutes.

2 Meanwhile, make the sauce. Put the honey into a non-stick pan and simmer until it turns a caramel color. Carefully pour in the vinegar and red wine and simmer until reduced by half. Add the soy sauce and reduce by half again, then add the stock and reduce by half once more. Season to taste with salt and pepper, being careful not to add too much salt because of the soy sauce. If it needs a little thickening, you could add a small piece of *beurre manié* (see Tips and Ideas, page 48). Whisk in the butter a few pieces at a time until smooth and adjust the seasoning if necessary.

3 Carve the duck and serve with the sauce and Roast Squash (see pages 196–197).

ROAST PARTRIDGE WITH PEARS

Partridge has such a short season that when you can get it you should make the most of it. This recipe is a great introduction to cooking game.

Serves 4

4 young partridges

olive oil

2 bacon slices, finely chopped

1 shallot, finely chopped

1 tablespoon redcurrant jelly

½ cup Poire Williams liqueur

2 cups chicken stock (see pages 30–31)

Beurre Manié (see Tips and Ideas, page 48), made with 0.5 ounces butter and 0.5 ounces flour

sea salt and black pepper

For the pears:

3 tablespoons unsalted butter

4 ripe pears, peeled, cored and finely sliced

2½ teaspoons superfine sugar

2½ teaspoons Poire Williams liqueur

1 First remove the wishbone from each partridge (see page 166), then season the birds with salt and pepper. Heat a large, heavy-bottomed frying pan, drizzle some oil into it and add the partridges. Brown the breasts for 30 seconds on each side, then turn the birds upright and transfer to a small roasting pan. Place in an oven preheated to 400°F and roast for 20 minutes. Remove from the oven and leave to rest while you make the sauce.

2 Heat a drizzle of olive oil in a frying pan, add the bacon and shallot and cook until soft. Stir in the redcurrant jelly, pour in the Poire Williams and simmer until slightly thickened and reduced. Add the chicken stock, return to a boil and simmer until reduced by half. Whisk in the *beurre manié* a small lump at a time to thicken the sauce; you may not need it all. Simmer for a few minutes until it thickens, then strain into a clean pan and season well.

3 For the pears, melt the butter in a large frying pan, add the pear slices and fry until beginning to color. Sprinkle on the sugar, cook for a few minutes longer, until lightly caramelized, then add the Poire Williams.

4 Put the partridges back into the oven to heat through for 2 minutes. Serve with the pears and sauce.

ROAST WHOLE SEA BASS WITH FENNEL, TOMATOES AND BASIL

A large fish lends itself very well to roasting. It's such an easy dish to do but so impressive. The only drawback is that serving it can be a little messy, but it tastes so good that that won't matter.

Serves 4

3 large fennel bulbs, thinly sliced

1 sea bass, weighing about 3½ pounds, scaled and cleaned

extra virgin olive oil

20 small cherry tomatoes

4 garlic cloves, finely chopped

20 basil leaves

sea salt and black pepper

1 Put the sliced fennel into a large baking dish big enough to hold the fish. Drizzle lightly with olive oil and shake to mix. Cover with foil and place in an oven preheated to 425°F. Bake for 30 minutes. Remove from the oven and gently stir in the tomatoes, garlic and basil leaves. Season well with salt and pepper.

2 Score the skin of the fish 2 or 3 times on each side along the body. Season well with salt and pepper and place on top of the fennel mixture. Drizzle with oil, then return the dish to the oven, uncovered, and roast for about 30 minutes. When the fish is done, a knife inserted near the backbone should come out easily. Serve with the fennel and tomatoes.

POT-ROAST CHICKEN WITH VEGETABLES

Pot-roasting chicken in a casserole with lots of vegetables keeps it lovely and moist because all the juices are retained. This works best with a small chicken, weighing about 3 pounds.

Serves 4

1 small chicken

olive oil

4 tablespoons soft unsalted butter

1 large onion, cut into slices about ½ inch thick

1 large leek, cut into slices about ½ inch thick

12 shallots, peeled, root trimmed but left attached

2 celery stalks, sliced

4 garlic cloves, cut into quarters

2 sprigs of thyme

1⅔ cups chicken stock (see pages 30–31)

sea salt and black pepper

chopped parsley, to garnish

1 Season the chicken with salt and pepper. Drizzle some oil into a frying pan over medium heat, add the chicken and brown it on all sides. Remove from the heat and leave to cool, then rub the chicken with the butter.

2 Put half the vegetables, the garlic and thyme in a casserole dish large enough to hold the chicken. Place the buttered chicken on top, put the rest of the vegetables around it in the dish, then pour in the stock and add some seasoning. Cover with a tight-fitting lid and transfer to an oven preheated to 375°F. Cook for 45 minutes, then remove and baste the bird well. Return to the oven for 35 minutes or until the chicken is cooked through (insert a knife in the thickest part of the thigh, near the bone, to check that the juices run clear).

3 Put the chicken on to a board and carve. Serve with the vegetables – I like to serve them in a large pasta bowl with the chicken on top, garnished with chopped parsley.

CASSEROLES *and* STEWS

Casseroles and stews are at the heart of home cooking. They are amazingly useful, as you can cook them in advance and then leave them sitting in the fridge for a couple of days until you want to eat them. Not only will they keep well but the flavor will actually mellow and improve. Don't think of casseroles as winter dishes only. Some of them, such as tagines and stifado, make perfect summer eating too.

Everybody loves a lamb tagine. The flavors are universal and it's a very easy dish to master, so it's worth making this the backbone of your repertoire.

TAGINE OF LAMB

SERVES 4–6

3½-pound boned shoulder of lamb, cut into 1-inch dice

about 5 tablespoons olive oil

1 onion, finely chopped

2 cups red wine

2½ tablespoons honey

1 tablespoon tomato paste

4 garlic cloves, finely chopped

¾-inch piece of fresh ginger, finely chopped

2½ teaspoons ground coriander

2½ teaspoons cumin seeds, crushed

5 teaspoons ground cinnamon

a good pinch of saffron strands

5 ounces raisins

2 ounces sliced almonds

1¼ cups chicken stock (see pages 30–31)

2 preserved lemons, skins only, finely sliced

7 tablespoons finely chopped cilantro

sea salt and black pepper

chopped flat-leaf parsley, to garnish

FOR THE COUSCOUS:

1½ cups chicken stock (see pages 30–31) or vegetable stock (see page 35) or water

a pinch of saffron strands (optional)

9 ounces couscous

1 Season the lamb with salt and pepper.

2 Heat the oil in a large casserole over a high heat and add the diced meat, cooking it in batches so you don't overcrowd the pan.

3 Fry the lamb until browned and caramelized all over.

4 Remove the lamb from the casserole and set aside.

5 Gently cook the onion in the same pan until softened, adding more oil if necessary.

6 Pour in the red wine.

7 Raise the heat and simmer until reduced by half, stirring and scraping the base of the pan with a wooden spoon to deglaze it.

8 Stir in the honey and tomato paste.

9 Return the lamb to the casserole with the garlic, ginger, spices, raisins and sliced almonds.

10 Pour in the chicken stock.

11 Stir well, then bring to a simmer and add some salt and pepper.

12 Cover the casserole and transfer to an oven preheated to 300°F. Cook for 2 hours or until the meat is very tender.

13 Remove from the oven and stir in the preserved lemon and cilantro. Adjust the seasoning, cover and set aside while you prepare the couscous.

14 To prepare the couscous, bring the stock or water to a boil and stir in the saffron, if using.

15 Put the couscous in a bowl.

16 Pour the hot stock or water over.

17 Then cover with plastic wrap and leave for 5 minutes.

18 Fluff up with a fork. Serve the tagine garnished with parsley and accompanied by the couscous.

TIPS AND IDEAS

■ When cooking meat for a casserole, it's important to sear it first – this adds flavor and also makes it look more attractive. Get a heavy-bottomed frying pan or a casserole very hot, add some oil, then season the meat and add to the pan – do this in batches, as if you squash it all in together, the meat will braise instead of fry. Get a good caramelized seal on the meat, turning it to brown on all sides.

■ Don't add too much liquid to casseroles – it should never come higher than the level of the meat. If it dries up too much, you can always add a little more as it cooks.

■ Fish casseroles needs a little more liquid and must not be stirred, otherwise they can end up as a mush. Unlike meat casseroles, they have only a very short cooking time.

■ Adding beans to vegetable casseroles gives them substance, but be sure to add plenty of flavor, too – garlic, chile, cilantro and soy sauce are all good.

■ Check meat casseroles occasionally during their long cooking time and stir to move the pieces around.

■ Meat casseroles and stews should be simmered very gently rather than boiled, or the meat can become tough.

■ Add chopped herbs to casseroles at the last minute to lift the flavor.

■ When seasoning casseroles, sometimes a little bit of sugar brings the flavor out.

■ To give a more refined finish to a casserole, you can remove the meat and vegetables at the end of the cooking period and then boil down the liquid to thicken it and concentrate the flavors. Strain the thickened liquid through a fine sieve, then return it to the pan, add the meat and vegetables and reheat gently. Add a little *beurre manié* if necessary (see Tips and Ideas, page 48) to thicken the sauce further.

■ Casseroles invariably taste better if made the day before and then reheated gently, as the flavors will have infused and the meat will have been rested.

■ Casseroles will keep well in the fridge for two or three days. Be careful when freezing them, though: if they contain root vegetables, they can become mushy. If necessary, remove the vegetables and just freeze the rest.

tagine variations

Lamb and Chickpea Tagine – drain a can of chickpeas and add the chickpeas to the tagine with the chicken stock.

Lamb and Apricot Tagine – replace the raisins with 5 ounces dried apricots, cut into quarters.

Chicken Tagine – replace the lamb with a large chicken, cut into 8 portions, browning it as on pages 172–174. Reduce the cooking time to 45 minutes.

Chicken and Pork Tagine – replace the lamb with a chicken, cut into 8 portions, and 1 pork tenderloin, cut into chunks. Brown them in oil, as above. Reduce the cooking time to 45 minutes.

LAMB AND WHITE BEAN CASSEROLE

This casserole is a classic French dish. I prefer to cut the meat into large pieces rather than leave the shoulder whole.

Serves 6

9 ounces white beans, soaked in cold water overnight

2¼ pounds boned shoulder of lamb, skin on, cut into 2½-inch cubes

olive oil

1 large onion, sliced

1 large carrot, sliced

2 garlic cloves, finely chopped

2 tablespoons thyme leaves

2 bay leaves

about 1⅔ cups chicken stock (see pages 30–31)

sea salt and black pepper

2½ tablespoons chopped parsley, to garnish

1 Drain the white beans, put them into a large pan and cover with fresh water. Bring to a boil, then reduce the heat and simmer for an hour. Remove from the heat and set aside.

2 Season the meat with salt and pepper. Heat some olive oil in a large, heavy-bottomed frying pan and brown the meat in it over a medium heat, cooking it in batches so as not to overcrowd the pan. Remove the meat from the pan and set aside.

3 Heat some more olive oil in a large, heavy-bottomed casserole, add the onion, carrot and garlic and cook gently for 5 minutes, until soft. Add the meat, thyme and bay leaves and then pour in enough stock to sit just level with the meat. Bring to a simmer, season well, then cover and place in an oven preheated to 325°F. Cook for 1 hour. Remove the casserole from the oven and skim off the fat from the surface. Drain the beans and add them to the casserole. Mix well and put it back in the oven for another hour, until the beans and lamb are very tender. Season well and serve sprinkled with parsley.

BEEF BOURGUIGNON

A traditional beef Bourguignon is made with good Burgundy wine, but don't worry if you can't find one — just use any wine you would drink yourself.

Serves 4

2¼ pounds chuck steak, cut into 1-inch cubes

3½ tablespoons all-purpose flour, seasoned with salt and pepper, for dusting

olive oil

7 ounces bacon, finely diced

2 garlic cloves, chopped

1 bottle of red wine

1 bouquet garni, made of 1 bay leaf, 2–3 sprigs of thyme and a few parsley stalks, enclosed in 2 pieces of celery stalk and tied with string

about 1½ cups beef stock (see page 34)

20 shallots

4¼ cups chicken stock (see pages 30–31)

2 tablespoons unsalted butter

9 ounces button mushrooms

sea salt and black pepper

chopped parsley, to garnish

1 Dust the pieces of beef in the seasoned flour. Heat some oil in a large, heavy-bottomed frying pan, add the beef and brown on all sides over medium heat, cooking it in batches to prevent overcrowding the pan. Transfer the beef to a large casserole. Fry the bacon in the pan until lightly colored and add to the casserole. Now soften the garlic in the pan and add that to the casserole too.

2 Pour the wine into the frying pan and add the bouquet garni. Bring to a boil, simmer for 1 minute and then add to the casserole. Mix well and add enough beef stock to come almost to the level of the beef. Cover and place in an oven preheated to 400°F. Cook for 30 minutes, then turn the oven down to 300°F and cook for another 2 hours, stirring once or twice.

3 To cook the shallots, first peel them carefully so they stay whole, then simmer them in the chicken stock for 10 minutes, until just tender. Remove with a slotted spoon, dry well, then brown in a frying pan in the butter and 2 1/2 tablespoons of olive oil until pale gold. Remove from the heat and set aside. Add the mushrooms to the stock and simmer for 5 minutes, then drain well (you can keep the stock and reuse it for something else) and add to the shallots.

4 Remove the casserole from the oven, add the shallots and mushrooms and season well. Take out and discard the bouquet garni. Return the casserole to the oven for 20 minutes, then serve garnished with chopped parsley.

BEEF GOULASH

If you want to save time, it's fine to use preroasted peppers from a jar and canned tomatoes in this warming recipe.

Serves 4

2 ounces all-purpose flour

1¾ pounds stew beef, cut into 1-inch cubes

olive oil

9 ounces onions, sliced

2 garlic cloves, finely chopped

4 ounces bacon, cut into strips

2½ tablespoons sweet paprika

½ teaspoon ground pie spice

½ cup red wine

14 ounces tomatoes, skinned, deseeded and chopped (see page 135)

1½ cups beef stock (see page 34)

2 red peppers

2½ tablespoons finely chopped parsley

⅔ cup sour cream

sea salt and black pepper

1 Put the flour into a large bowl and season well with salt and pepper. Toss in the cubes of beef so they become coated with the flour.

2 Put a drizzle of olive oil in a large frying pan and place over a high heat. Add the meat and brown it on all sides – do this in batches so as not to overcrowd the pan – then transfer it to a large casserole when it is done. Now reduce the heat, add a little more oil to the frying pan if necessary and fry the onions until lightly browned. Add them to the beef with the garlic. Finally cook the bacon until browned, adding that to the beef too.

3 Mix the beef in the casserole with the paprika and mixed spice, place over the heat and cook for 1 minute. Add the red wine, chopped tomatoes and stock, give everything a good stir and bring to a boil. Season with salt and pepper, cover and transfer to an oven preheated to 350°F. Cook for 45 minutes, then reduce the temperature to 300°F and cook for another 1 1/2 hours, until the meat is tender. Check after about an hour that the casserole hasn't become too dry, and add a little more stock or water if necessary.

4 In the meantime put the peppers under a hot grill or directly on a gas burner and leave until blackened and blistered all over, turning occasionally. Cool slightly, then skin and deseed the peppers and cut the flesh into strips.

5 When the beef is done, stir in the red peppers and adjust the seasoning. Serve garnished with the parsley, accompanied by the sour cream and some basmati rice (see page 120).

STIFADO

The flavor of this classic Greek stew should be very intense and tomatoey, so you need to make sure the liquid is well reduced. Serving it with feta cheese gives it that extra richness. There are a lot of shallots to peel here. A useful tip is to put them in boiling water for a minute before peeling, then the skins come off easily.

Serves 6

olive oil

3½ pounds sirloin steak, cut into 1½-inch cubes

1 onion, chopped

3 garlic cloves, chopped

1 dried bay leaf, crumbled

3 x 2-inch cinnamon sticks

3½ tablespoons red wine vinegar

1 cup red wine

3½ cups hot chicken stock (see pages 30–31)

24 small shallots, peeled, root left on

3 tablespoons unsalted butter

¾ cup tomato paste

1 teaspoon sugar

9 ounces feta cheese, crumbled

sea salt and black pepper

2½ tablespoons chopped parsley, to garnish

1 Drizzle some oil in a large, heavy-bottomed casserole and place over the heat. Season the meat with salt and pepper, then brown it in the oil over medium heat, cooking it in batches so as not to crowd the pan. Remove from the pan and set aside. Add the onion and garlic to the pan and cook gently until softened. Return the beef to the pan, stir in the bay leaf, cinnamon, vinegar and wine, cover tightly and transfer to an oven preheated to 325°F. Cook for 30 minutes, then pour in the hot chicken stock and return the casserole to the oven for 1 hour.

2 Meanwhile, cook the shallots in a pan of simmering water for 5 minutes, then drain well. Melt the butter in a frying pan, add the shallots and fry until lightly glazed all over. Add them to the casserole with the tomato paste and sugar, return to the oven and cook for 1 hour or until the meat is tender.

3 Remove the meat and shallots from the pan with a slotted spoon and place in a bowl. Put the casserole on the stovetop and boil until the liquid reduces and the flavor has intensified. Season to taste with salt and pepper, then return the meat and shallots to the pan. Divide between 6 serving bowls, sprinkle on the feta, garnish with parsley and serve.

LAMB HOTPOT

Lamb hotpot is an old-fashioned dish that deserves to be eaten more often. It is the most delicious meal but uses such simple ingredients. I like to make it with leg of lamb.

Serves 4

5 tablespoons unsalted butter

2 leeks, finely chopped

1 onion, sliced

2 garlic cloves, finely chopped

about 1¾ pounds leg of lamb, divided into chop-size pieces

2½ tablespoons all-purpose flour, seasoned with salt and pepper, for dusting

olive oil

1¾ pounds waxy potatoes, peeled and finely sliced

4 sprigs of thyme

2 cups chicken stock (see pages 30–31)

sea salt and black pepper

1 Melt 3 tablespoons of the butter in a large frying pan, add the leeks, onion and garlic and cook gently for about 5 minutes, until softened. Remove from the pan, divide into 2 piles and put to one side.

2 Dust the lamb in seasoned flour. Drizzle some oil into the frying pan, add a knob of the remaining butter, then add the lamb and brown it on both sides.

3 Mix half the leeks and onion with half the sliced potatoes and season well with salt and pepper. Arrange this mixture in a large, heavy-bottomed casserole. Season the remaining leek and onion mixture and layer it with the lamb and thyme in the casserole, on top of the potatoes. Pour on the stock and season well. Finally, season the remaining potatoes and layer them on top of the lamb so you end up with a spiral of potato.

4 Dot the potatoes with the remaining butter, cover the casserole and place in an oven preheated to 400°F. Cook for 30 minutes, then reduce the heat to 300°F and cook for 1 hour. Remove the lid and cook for another 45 minutes, until the lamb is cooked through and the potatoes are very tender.

NORMANDY CHICKEN

Serves 4

1 chicken, cut into 4 portions

all-purpose flour, seasoned with salt and pepper, for dusting

olive oil

5 tablespoons unsalted butter

20 shallots, peeled, root left on

1 cup chicken stock (see pages 30–31)

1 cup dry hard cider

3 tart eating apples, preferably Granny Smith, cored and thinly sliced (but not peeled)

⅔ cup heavy cream

8 sage leaves, chopped

sea salt and black pepper

1 Dust the chicken pieces in seasoned flour. Heat some olive oil in a large, heavy-bottomed frying pan, add the chicken and brown on all sides over a medium heat. Transfer to a large casserole.

2 Melt half the butter and a tablespoon of oil in the frying pan and add the shallots. Cook gently for about 10 minutes, until softened. Stir in a tablespoon of flour, cook for 1 minute, then pour in half the chicken stock. Bring to a simmer, mix thoroughly and add to the chicken pieces in the casserole. Pour the cider and the rest of the chicken stock into the frying pan, bring to a boil and stir well. Add to the casserole, mix well and place in an oven preheated to 350°F. Cook for 45–50 minutes, until the chicken is tender.

3 Melt the remaining butter in a large frying pan, toss in the apple slices and cook until lightly colored. Stir the apples into the casserole with the cream and sage, and check the seasoning. Return to the oven for 10 minutes, then serve, accompanied by boiled or steamed rice.

MEDITERRANEAN FISH CASSEROLE

Fish casseroles are so quick to do. You can cook the vegetables in advance, then shortly before you are ready to serve, add the fish and stock and complete the cooking.

Serves 4

olive oil

1 fennel bulb, sliced lengthwise

1 Spanish onion, sliced

1 red pepper, sliced lengthwise

2 garlic cloves, chopped

7 ounces haddock fillet, skinned and cut into chunks

7 ounces sea bass fillet, skinned and cut into chunks

7 ounces large raw shrimp, peeled (use the tip of a sharp knife to remove the black vein running down the back of each one)

7 ounces ripe tomatoes, skinned and deseeded (see page 135), then cut into eighths

3 sprigs of thyme

2 sprigs of marjoram

a large pinch of saffron strands

6½ cups hot fish stock (see page 35) or chicken stock (see pages 30–31)

sea salt and black pepper

chopped parsley, to garnish

1 Heat some olive oil in a large casserole, add the fennel and onion and cook gently until soft. This can take up to 15 minutes. Transfer to a plate, add the red pepper and garlic to the casserole and cook until soft.

2 Return the fennel and onion to the casserole, along with the fish, prawns, tomatoes, thyme, marjoram and saffron, and mix together gently. Season well, cover with the hot stock and bring to a simmer. Do not stir. Cook gently for about 15 minutes, until the fish is tender. Serve in large bowls, sprinkled with chopped parsley and accompanied by boiled or steamed new potatoes.

CHILI CON CARNE

There is endless controversy about what constitutes a proper chili. My version is a little unusual because it is baked, rather than cooked on top of the stove, which I find gives it a particularly intense flavor.

Serves 4

2½ tablespoons olive oil

2 onions, finely chopped

2 garlic cloves, finely chopped

21 ounces finely minced beef

21 ounces tomatoes, skinned, deseeded and chopped (see page 135) or a 14-ounce can of tomatoes

1 teaspoon hot chili powder, or to taste

2½ teaspoons ground cumin

about 2 cups beef stock (see page 34)

1 can of kidney beans, drained

1 tablespoon tomato paste

sea salt and black pepper

To serve:

⅔ cup sour cream

3½ tablespoons cilantro leaves

1 Heat the oil in a large casserole, add the onions and garlic and cook gently until softened. Turn the heat up, add the beef and cook until lightly browned, separating the strands of beef with a fork to prevent lumps.

2 Add the tomatoes, chili, cumin, stock and some salt and pepper and bring to the boil. Cover and place in an oven preheated to 400°F. Cook for 25 minutes, then turn the heat down to 300°F and stir in the kidney beans. Cook for a further 1 1/2 hours, giving it a good stir every 30 minutes and checking to make sure it isn't getting dry – add a little more stock if necessary.

3 Remove the casserole from the oven and stir in the tomato paste. Adjust the seasoning and serve topped with the sour cream and cilantro and accompanied by boiled rice (see page 120).

COTTAGE PIE

Serves 4

2½ tablespoons olive oil

2 onions, finely chopped

3 garlic cloves, finely chopped

21 ounces finely minced beef

10 ounces tomatoes, skinned, deseeded and chopped (see page 135) or a 7-ounce can of tomatoes

1 teaspoon chopped thyme

about 1½ cups beef stock (see page 34)

2½ tablespoons tomato paste

2 teaspoons sugar

1½ pounds potatoes

½ cup milk

3½ tablespoons butter

freshly grated nutmeg

sea salt and black pepper

1 Heat the oil in a large casserole that can go on the stovetop, add the onions and garlic and cook until softened. Turn the heat up, add the beef and cook until lightly browned, separating the strands of beef with a fork to prevent lumps.

2 Add the tomatoes, thyme, stock, sugar, and some salt and pepper and bring to the boil. Cover and place in an oven preheated to 400°F. Cook for 25 minutes, then turn the heat down to 300°F. Cook for a further 45 minutes, giving it a good stir half way through cooking and checking to make sure it isn't getting dry.

3 Remove the casserole from the oven, put on the stovetop and remove the lid. Stir in the tomato paste and adjust the seasoning. Cook on a low heat for 20 minutes to thicken it. Allow to cool.

4 While the casserole is cooling, cook the potatoes in boiling salted water until tender, then drain thoroughly and mash with the milk, butter and some salt, pepper and grated nutmeg.

5 Top the casserole with the mashed potato and dot with a little butter. Bake at 400°F for about 20 minutes, until lightly browned.

VEGETABLE AND BUTTERBEAN STEW WITH TOMATOES

This is an old favorite of mine. You can eat it hot — on its own or with
pork or lamb chops — or cold as a summer dish. Chickpeas and white beans
would work well instead of butterbeans.

Serves 4

14 ounces dried butterbeans, soaked in cold
water overnight

½ cup extra virgin olive oil

2½ tablespoons tomato paste

4 garlic cloves, finely chopped

2 bay leaves

2 sprigs of thyme

2 red peppers

1 large eggplant, cut into ¾-inch dice

1 onion, sliced

18 ounces tomatoes, skinned, deseeded and
roughly chopped (see page 135)

1 teaspoon sugar

1 tablespoon chopped basil

sea salt and black pepper

1 Drain the beans, put them into a large pan and
cover generously with cold water. Bring to a boil,
then reduce the heat and simmer for about an hour,
until the beans are almost, but not quite, tender.
Strain and reserve the liquid. Put the beans into a
large casserole or earthenware dish and add half the
olive oil, plus the tomato paste, garlic, bay leaves
and thyme. Leave to one side while you prepare the
vegetables.

2 Place the red peppers under a hot broiler or directly
on a gas burner and leave until blackened and
blistered all over, turning occasionally. Cool slightly,
then skin and deseed the peppers and cut the flesh
into strips.

3 Heat the remaining olive oil in a large, heavy-
bottomed frying pan, add the diced eggplant and
cook over a fairly high heat until lightly browned on
all sides. Add the eggplant to the butterbeans. Add a
little more oil to the pan, if necessary, add the onion
and cook gently until softened. Stir in the chopped
tomatoes and bring to a simmer, then add the sugar
and some salt and pepper and cook for 5 minutes.
Add this mixture to the beans.

4 Add the strips of pepper to the beans. Mix all the
ingredients in the casserole well and add a little of
the reserved bean cooking water – not enough to
cover the mixture but just to thin it slightly. Cover
the casserole, place it in an oven preheated to 400°F
and cook for 45 minutes. Stir in the chopped basil,
adjust the seasoning and serve.

VEGETABLES

I absolutely love vegetables. My mother had her own vegetable garden and, from a very early age, I was growing and picking my own fava beans and runner beans. However, I am a firm believer in the importance of eating vegetables in season, when they are at their most flavorful. This chapter focuses on simple cooking methods that will really bring out the best in your vegetables.

This is a particularly luxurious mash recipe, made with a lot of butter and whole milk — but it's worth it. This is comfort food at its best.

～ MASHED POTATO ～

SERVES 4

2¼ pounds starchy potatoes

7 tablespoons unsalted butter, diced

1¼ cups whole milk

sea salt and white pepper

TIPS AND IDEAS

■ There are lots of interesting potato varieties today, so try experimenting with your mash. Starchy potatoes, which disintegrate easily, are traditional for mash and also make the best roast potatoes.

■ Don't overcook the potatoes or the mash will be watery. On the other hand, if you undercook them, they will taste starchy and horrible.

■ When adding milk to mash, always use hot rather than cold milk. It will be absorbed more easily.

■ For the smoothest, fluffiest mash, use a stainless-steel potato ricer rather than a masher. It looks like a giant garlic press, and you simply put the potatoes into the ricer compartment and press down with the handle – perfect, lump-free mash is pushed out through lots of tiny holes. I also use a drum sieve (tamis) for mash, or you can use an ordinary fine-mesh sieve.

■ If you want to use the mash to make potato cakes, mash them without any butter and milk.

1 Peel the potatoes and cut them into roughly equal chunks, so they cook evenly.

2 Put them into a large saucepan, cover with cold water, season with salt and bring to the boil.

3 Reduce the heat and simmer, uncovered, for 15–20 minutes, until the potatoes are very tender but not falling apart.

4 Test them with the point of a knife – if it slips in easily, they are done.

5 Drain well and leave in the colander for a couple of minutes to steam off excess moisture.

6 Return the potatoes to the pan and add the butter.

7 Then mash the potatoes well (or you can put them through a potato ricer into the pan and then mix in the butter).

8 Heat the milk in a small pan until very hot, but not boiling.

9 Gradually add the milk to the mashed potato, beating well with a wooden spoon. Season with salt and white pepper and serve immediately.

Mashes and purées

Saffron Mashed Potato – follow the recipe on pages 188–189, adding a large pinch of saffron strands to the milk when you heat it. This will give the mash a lovely yellow glow.

Chive Mashed Potato – follow the recipe on pages 188–189, adding 7 tablespoons of finely chopped chives at the end.

Potato Purée – follow the recipe on pages 188–189, putting the potatoes through a potato ricer or a fine sieve rather than using a masher, so they are really silky. Increase the milk to 2 cups.

Root Vegetable Purée – take 7 ounces each of peeled and chopped celeriac, carrots and parsnips, making sure they are cut into pieces of roughly equal size. Cook in boiling salted water until very soft, then drain thoroughly. Put in a food processor with 3.5 ounces unsalted butter and process until smooth (you may have to do this in 2 batches). Reheat gently in a clean saucepan and stir in ¼ cup heavy cream and some sea salt and white pepper.

Celeriac Purée – peel 1¾ pounds celeriac and cut into ¾-inch dice. Put it into a large saucepan and pour in 2 cups whole milk, topping it up with water, if necessary, so the celeriac is just covered. Add a sprig of rosemary and simmer for 20 minutes, until the celeriac is very tender. Discard the rosemary and drain the celeriac, reserving some of the liquid. Purée the celeriac in a food processor with 3.5 ounces unsalted butter, adding a little of the reserved cooking liquid if the purée is too stiff. Season with salt, pepper and a teaspoon of sugar, reheat gently and serve.

BOILING VEGETABLES

There are two simple rules for boiling vegetables: root vegetables should be added to cold salted water, while greens and beans go into boiling salted water. Root vegetables must be brought to a boil in enough water just to cover, then simmered till tender – a knife should come out easily when inserted. Drain them very thoroughly, then leave them in a colander for a few minutes to steam off the excess moisture, or even put them on a cloth.

Add green vegetables to just enough boiling salted water to cover them. Make sure the pan is large enough – the vegetables need room to move around as they cook. Always undercook them slightly, but make sure they are not too *al dente*. The best thing to do after draining green vegetables is to refresh them in cold water and then reheat gently in butter just before serving, either on the stove top or in the oven. This is very convenient for the cook as it means you don't need to cook everything at the last minute.

STEAMING VEGETABLES

Steaming is a great way to cook vegetables, as the flavor is not diluted. It also retains all the nutrients, making it one of the healthiest cooking methods. I am not keen on tiered steamers – you get more even results if you cook one layer at a time. As with boiled vegetables, keep them quite *al dente*. Keep the water in the base of your steamer at a simmer, so you cook the vegetables gently, and check it occasionally to make sure it doesn't run dry. Once the vegetables are done to your liking, drain them well – some vegetables contain a lot of water. Leave them on a cloth to dry if necessary.

This is a delicious but rich dish. Don't hold back with the cream, and even add a little bit more if you think it needs it. Also, take the time to layer the potatoes properly, so the gratin will look as good as it tastes.

GRATIN DAUPHINOIS

SERVES 4

1 ½ cups heavy cream

½ cup whole milk

2 garlic cloves, finely chopped

1 ½ tablespoons unsalted butter

2 ½ pounds starchy potatoes

2.5 ounces Gruyère or Emmenthal cheese, grated (optional)

sea salt and white pepper

1 Put the cream, milk and garlic into a saucepan.

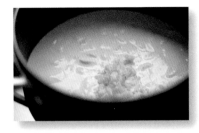

2 Bring to a boil and then remove from the heat.

3 Season the cream generously; it should taste very salty. The salty taste will be diluted by the potatoes.

4 Use most of the butter to grease an ovenproof gratin dish about 9½ x 6 inches.

5 Peel the potatoes.

6 Slice them very thinly; you can use a mandoline, a large, sharp knife or the slicing attachment of a food processor for this.

7 Start arranging the potatoes in overlapping rows in the dish.

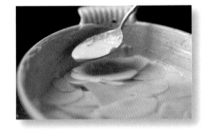

8 Pour a little of the infused cream over each layer.

9 Continue until all the potatoes and cream have been added, finishing with cream.

10 Dot the top with the remaining butter, cover with foil, then place in an oven preheated to 325°F and bake for 1½ hours.

11 Remove the dish from the oven and press the potatoes down so they are submerged in the cream. Sprinkle over the cheese, if using.

12 Return to the oven and cook, uncovered, for about 30 minutes, until the potatoes are very tender. Leave to rest for 10 minutes and then serve.

dauphinois variations

Turnip and Potato Dauphinois – follow the recipe on pages 192–193, replacing half the potatoes with turnips and using all cream rather than cream and milk.

Celeriac and Potato Dauphinois – follow the recipe on pages 192–193, replacing half the potatoes with celeriac and using all cream rather than cream and milk.

Jerusalem Artichoke and Potato Dauphinois – follow the recipe on pages 192–193, replacing about a third of the potatoes with Jerusalem artichokes. To prevent the artichokes from discoloring, put them in a bowl of water containing the juice of 1 lemon as you peel them.

Saffron or Cumin Dauphinois – follow the recipe on pages 192–193, adding a pinch of saffron strands, 2½ teaspoons of ground cumin or 1 rounded teaspoon of cumin seeds to the cream and milk.

Pommes Boulangère – follow the recipe on pages 192–193, adding layers of very finely sliced onion to the dish.

TIPS AND IDEAS

■ Seasoning is very important with gratins – season the liquid very generously, so the sauce will flavor the vegetables.

■ If you make a gratin with vegetables that have a low starch content, such as celeriac and Jerusalem artichokes, you need to layer them with some potatoes, otherwise they won't stick together.

■ Traditionally gratins are cooked in a shallow dish but I like them slightly deeper than usual – about 1 1/2–2 inches high.

■ Gratins need to be cooked slowly. The top should be golden rather than dark brown.

■ The wonderful thing about a gratin is that you can take it to the table in its dish for people to help themselves.

■ For a lighter gratin, substitute chicken stock (see pages 30–31) for the cream.

■ Unfortunately gratins do not freeze well. However, you can assemble a gratin the day before and keep it in the fridge, then cook it when you need it.

If you're in a hurry, you can leave the skin on when roasting butternut squash, as it is quite tender and easy to eat. Other squashes need to be peeled before roasting.

ROAST SQUASH

SERVES 4

1 butternut squash, weighing about 2¼ pounds

8 sprigs of thyme

2½ tablespoons olive oil

sea salt and black pepper

1 Peel the squash.

2 Cut the squash in half.

3 Remove the seeds and any stringy bits from the squash.

4 Now cut the squash into wedges about 2 inches x ¾ inch.

5 Place in a roasting pan with the sprigs of thyme and some salt and pepper.

6 Add the olive oil and mix well. Place in an oven preheated to 400°F and roast for 40–45 minutes, turning the pieces halfway through.

Roast vegetable variations

Roast Potatoes – peel about 2½ pounds starchy potatoes, cut them into large pieces and cook in boiling salted water for 8 minutes, until half done. Drain well and then shake in a colander to roughen up the edges slightly (this makes them fluffy when roasted). Put 3½ tablespoons of olive oil, goose fat or drippings into a roasting pan large enough to hold the potatoes in a single layer and put it in an oven preheated to 400°F for a good 5 minutes, until very hot. Add the well-drained potatoes and turn them to coat them in the oil. Roast for about 45 minutes, shaking the pan gently every 15 minutes, until the potatoes are crisp and golden on the outside, tender and fluffy inside. Sprinkle with coarse sea salt, shake again and return to the oven for 5 minutes.

Roast Parsnips – peel 4 parsnips, cut them into 2-inch x ¾-inch lengths and put them in a roasting dish with 2 tablespoons melted butter, 1 tablespoon of olive oil and some salt and pepper. Mix well, then put them in an oven preheated to 400°F and roast for 1 hour, shaking the dish every 15 minutes. Add 2½ tablespoons of runny honey and toss carefully. Return the dish to the oven, turning the heat up to 425°F and cook for 15–20 minutes, until tender, browned and lightly caramelized.

Roast Carrots – this is a wonderful way of cooking carrots because it brings out their sweetness. I like using whole new carrots with a little bit of the stalk still attached; otherwise sticks will do. Cut 21 ounces carrots into sticks about 2½ inches x ¾ inch and toss them with 1 teaspoon of coarse sea salt, 1½ tablespoons melted butter and 2½ tablespoons olive oil. Put them into a roasting pan in a single layer and roast at 400°F for about 45 minutes, turning them halfway through. When they have been cooking for 30 minutes, you can sprinkle them with a teaspoon of sugar, if you like, which gives a delicious caramelized result.

Roast Shallots – peel 18 ounces medium shallots, trimming the root but leaving it attached (it is easier to peel shallots if you put them in boiling water for a couple of minutes first). Don't cut the tops, but leave them with a point, which will help them stay intact during roasting. Put the shallots in a roasting dish and dot 2 tablespoons unsalted butter over the top. Drizzle with olive oil and season with salt and pepper. Mix well and then roast in an oven preheated to 350°F for 45 minutes, shaking the dish every 15 minutes. Sprinkle with 1 teaspoon of sugar and roast for another 15 minutes.

Roast Beets – I love roast baby beets and they are very easy to do. Cut the stalks off 25 ounces beets, leaving a tiny bit still protruding. Put them on a large piece of foil, dot with 2 tablespoons butter and drizzle with 2 tablespoons of olive oil. Season with salt and pepper and mix well. Pull up the foil round the beets and fold the edges to seal, making a loose parcel. Roast in an oven preheated to 400°F for about 1½ hours, shaking the parcel every 15 minutes, until the beets are tender when pierced with a knife. Rub off the skins and serve. If you can't get baby beets, cut larger ones into quarters before cooking.

Roast Tomatoes with Garlic and Thyme – in a large bowl, mix together ⅓ cup extra virgin olive oil, 3 finely chopped garlic cloves, 3½ teaspoons of dried thyme, 2½ teaspoons of coarse sea salt and some black pepper. Cut 1¼ pounds medium vine-ripened tomatoes in half and remove the seeds. Stir the tomatoes into the oil until they are thoroughly coated, then place them cut side down on a baking sheet. Bake in an oven preheated to 375°F for 30–35 minutes, until the tomatoes are very soft but just holding their shape.

POTATO WEDGES

You can flavor these by mixing in a little chopped garlic, rosemary or thyme with the oil and salt. I also like to add quartered lemons, or sprinkle sesame seeds on top for a great texture.

Serves 4

6 starchy potatoes

5 tablespoons olive oil

sea salt

1 Scrub the potatoes but don't peel them. Cut them into wedges and put them into a bowl. Sprinkle with olive oil and sea salt and mix well with your hands.

2 Spread the potatoes out on a baking sheet and place in an oven preheated to 425°F. Bake for 30 minutes, then turn the wedges over and cook for another 30 minutes, turning once or twice more, until the wedges are crisp and golden. Sprinkle with a little more salt if necessary and serve immediately.

BUTTERNUT SQUASH AND CUMIN PURÉE

Thinned with chicken or vegetable stock, this also makes a very good soup.

Serves 4

1 large butternut squash, weighing about 2¼ pounds, peeled, deseeded and cut into ¾-inch pieces

3½ tablespoons unsalted butter, diced

2½ teaspoons cumin seeds, crushed

1 garlic clove, finely chopped

½ cup heavy cream

sea salt and white pepper

1 Take a large double layer of foil and put it into an ovenproof dish. Fill with the butternut squash, butter, crushed cumin seeds, garlic and some salt and pepper. Wrap up loosely, put into an oven preheated to 325°F and bake for 1 1/2 hours or until the squash is tender.

2 Remove from the oven and put everything into a food processor and purée until smooth. Transfer to a clean saucepan and add the heavy cream. Heat for about a minute, until slightly thickened, then adjust the seasoning and serve.

PEA, MINT AND GOAT CHEESE PURÉE

Peas make such a lovely, summery purée and this one goes with so many things — fish, pork and chicken are particularly good.

Serves 4

2 tablespoons unsalted butter

5 ounces onions, finely chopped

1 pound frozen peas, cooked

5 tablespoons soft, fresh goat cheese

a pinch of cayenne pepper

1 teaspoon sugar

15 mint leaves

a little vegetable stock (see page 35), if needed

sea salt and black pepper

Melt the butter in a frying pan, add the onions and cook until soft but not browned. Stir in the cooked peas, then transfer to a food processor and add the goat cheese, cayenne, sugar and mint. Purée until smooth. You may need to loosen the purée a little by adding some vegetable stock, but be careful not to put too much in. Season well with salt and pepper, then transfer to a saucepan and reheat gently.

SAUTÉED CARROTS

This is one of my favorite ways of cooking carrots. You need to have patience and cook them slowly, keeping all the flavors in rather than boiling them out.

Serves 4

3 tablespoons unsalted butter

olive oil

1½ pounds carrots, peeled and cut into 2½-inch x ¾-inch sticks

2½ tablespoons finely chopped parsley

sea salt and white pepper

Melt the butter in a large, non-stick frying pan with a drizzle of olive oil. Add the carrots and cook over a low heat for 45 minutes, until tender and very lightly caramelized, turning frequently. Season well with salt and pepper. The carrots can be cooked several hours in advance up to this point and then reheated. Toss in the parsley and serve.

Other sautés

Sautéed Zucchini – cut 1½ pounds zucchini into rounds ⅛-inch thick. Cook them in the butter and oil over a fairly high heat until they start to brown. Add 1 finely chopped garlic clove, plus 2½ tablespoons of chopped tarragon, if you like, season with salt and pepper and cook, turning frequently for 5 minutes. Serve immediately.

Sautéed Asparagus – break the woody base off 18 ounces asparagus spears. Melt the butter and oil, as above, let them get hot, then add the asparagus and reduce the heat. Cook for about 6 minutes, turning occasionally, until brown and tender, then season with coarse sea salt and serve. This is great with a fried egg.

Sautéed Spinach – remove any large stalks from 18–22 ounces fresh spinach. Melt 3 tablespoons unsalted butter in a large frying pan, then throw in the spinach. You may have to do this a handful at a time if the pan isn't large enough to contain it all, adding more as it wilts down. Toss over medium heat until all the spinach has wilted, then drain very thoroughly. Return to the pan with another 3 tablespoons butter, mix well, season to taste with salt and pepper and serve.

Sautéed Mushrooms – halve 1 pound button mushrooms and remove the stalks. Heat the butter and olive oil in a frying pan, as above, then throw in the mushrooms and turn the heat right up – they will exude a lot of liquid, which needs to be cooked off. Cook for about 5 minutes, stirring often, until tender, then season well with salt and pepper and serve.

BRAISED FENNEL

Braising is a method of cooking a vegetable slowly in a little liquid so it effectively steams in the dish, resulting in a wonderfully intense flavor. Almost any vegetable is suitable for this treatment.

Serves 8

4 fennel bulbs

2 tablespoons unsalted butter, melted

½ cup chicken stock (see pages 30–31)

5 tablespoons freshly grated Parmesan cheese

sea salt and black pepper

Cut each fennel bulb into quarters lengthways, leaving the root attached so the pieces don't fall apart. Place the fennel in a gratin dish in a single layer and brush the butter all over. Season well with salt and pepper, pour the stock over, then cover and place in an oven preheated to 300°F. Cook for 40 minutes, then uncover the dish and sprinkle the Parmesan over. Return to the oven for 20–30 minutes, until the fennel is very tender.

BRAISED RED CABBAGE WITH PEARS

Braised red cabbage is such a useful dish because it can be kept in the fridge for several days and reheated. It's very good with game or beef.

Serves 4–6

8 tablespoons unsalted butter

5 ounces onions, finely chopped

3 bacon slices, very finely diced

3 garlic cloves, finely chopped

1 red cabbage, finely sliced

½ cup red wine vinegar

¾ cup red wine (optional)

5 tablespoons honey

2 cups chicken stock (see pages 30–31)

2 pears, peeled, cored and finely diced

1½ teaspoons black pepper

sea salt

1 Melt 3 1/2 tablespoons of the butter in a large, heavy-based saucepan, add the onions and cook gently until softened but not browned. Add the bacon and garlic and continue cooking for a couple of minutes. Stir in the red cabbage, then add the vinegar and cook for 1 minute. Stir in the red wine, if using, plus the honey and chicken stock. Bring to a simmer, then cover the pan, reduce the heat and cook gently for 1 1/2 hours, stirring every 10 minutes.

2 Add the diced pears and black pepper and cook for another 40 minutes, until the cabbage is very soft. Leave to stand for 5 minutes, then drain off the juices. Add the rest of the butter for richness, then check the seasoning: it should taste peppery and sweet.

CRUSHED POTATO, ROSEMARY AND THYME CAKES

This wonderfully easy dish is delicious with roast chicken.

Serves 4

18 ounces small new potatoes, scrubbed

5 tablespoons extra virgin olive oil

1 teaspoon chopped rosemary

1 tablespoon chopped thyme

sea salt and black pepper

1 Cook the potatoes in boiling salted water until tender, then drain well. Put them back into the pan and crush them roughly with the back of a fork. Stir in the olive oil, rosemary and thyme and season well with salt and pepper, then leave to cool.

2 Place four 2 3/4-inch metal rings on an oiled baking tray and fill with the potato mixture. Place in an oven preheated to 350°F and bake for about 45 minutes, until crisp and brown. Remove the rings and serve.

POMMES ANNA

You might be alarmed at the amount of butter in this dish but it makes the potatoes meltingly soft, with a lovely crisp top.

Serves 6

2¼ pounds waxy potatoes, peeled

5 ounces unsalted butter, melted

sea salt and black pepper

1 Slice the potatoes very thinly on a mandoline or using the slicing attachment of a food processor. Use some of the butter to grease an 8-inch round gratin dish or any other round ovenproof dish, such as a cake pan, and line the base with a circle of baking parchment. Arrange the sliced potatoes neatly in the dish, drizzling each layer with the butter as you go and seasoning with salt and pepper.

2 Cover with a piece of buttered wax paper and put into an oven preheated to 350°F. Bake for about 1 1/2 hours, until the potatoes are very tender. Check with a knife, and if necessary return them to the oven for another 10 minutes. Unmold on to a plate and serve straight away.

PASTRY

In my cooking courses, pastry is the one thing that people invariably say they're frightened of making. The best advice I can give to anybody is to touch the pastry as little as possible, then it will be easier to work with. Have confidence, be positive and develop a light touch — your pastry will be deliciously crisp and delicate.

This is a good example of the importance of a perfect pastry shell, baked blind until golden and crisp. Once you've mastered the technique, there is no end to the fillings you can use. The classic way to make a quiche Lorraine is to simmer the Canadian bacon rather than fry it, but I like to soften it in a little olive oil. This recipe may look very rich but you only need a small slice and it tastes wonderful.

QUICHE LORRAINE

To make the basic Shortcrust Pastry, follow steps 1 to 7
To blind bake a pastry case, follow steps 14 to 18

SERVES 6–8

1 tablespoon olive oil

7 ounces smoked Canadian bacon, cut into small pieces

2 eggs

2 egg yolks

3.5 ounces Cheddar cheese, finely grated

1½ cups heavy cream (or use half whipping cream, half heavy)

sea salt and black pepper

FOR THE SHORTCRUST PASTRY:

9 ounces all-purpose flour

½ teaspoon salt

9 tablespoons chilled unsalted butter, cut into small cubes

2 egg yolks

3½–5 tablespoons cold water

1 First make the pastry. Sift the flour and salt into a large bowl.

2 Add the cubed butter and rub it into the flour with your fingertips until the mixture resembles fine breadcrumbs.

3 Mix the egg yolks in a small bowl with 3½ tablespoons of water.

4 Pour the egg yolks into the center of the flour mixture.

5 Stir with a round-bladed knife or a fork to bring everything together into a fairly firm, smooth dough. If it is too dry, add the remaining water.

6 Knead lightly for a few seconds to make it homogenous.

7 Then shape the dough into a cylinder, wrap in plastic wrap and put into the fridge for at least 30 minutes.

8 Using a rolling pin, roll the pastry out on a lightly floured surface to a circle about ⅛-inch thick.

9 Use to line a 9-inch removable-bottomed tart pan, about 1½ inches deep: carefully fold the pastry circle into four, making a triangle.

10 Put the corner in the center of the tart pan. Then unfold the pastry, making sure you get it right into the edges of the pan.

11 Take a ball of the excess pastry the size of a walnut, wrap it in plastic wrap and use it to press the pastry well into the edges of the pan.

12 Once the pastry is lining the pan snugly and overlapping the edges, run the rolling pin lightly over the top of the pan to cut off the excess pastry.

13 With your thumbs, press the pastry gently up the sides of the pan so it comes about ¼ inch above the top. Put it into the fridge for 30 minutes.

14 Now you need to bake the pastry blind. Remove the pastry shell from the fridge and prick the base lightly all over with a fork.

15 Take a large piece of baking parchment and scrunch it up, then unfold it and use to line the pastry shell, covering the base and sides.

16 Fill the pastry shell right to the top with baking beans or with rice or ordinary dried beans – you can keep them and re-use them endlessly.

17 Place the pan on a hot baking sheet in an oven preheated to 400°F and bake for 15–20 minutes, until the pastry is dry to the touch.

18 Remove the rice or beans and paper and return to the oven for 5 minutes, until the base is lightly colored. Remove from the oven and set aside.

19 To make the filling, heat the olive oil in a frying pan. Add the Canadian bacon and cook gently for a few minutes, but do not let it brown.

20 Remove from the heat, drain off the fat from the Canadian bacon and leave to cool.

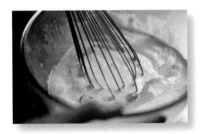

21 Lightly whisk the eggs, egg yolks, Cheddar and cream together and season well with salt and pepper.

22 Put the bacon in the pastry shell.

23 Pour in the cream mixture. Put the quiche straight into the oven at 400°F and cook for 15 minutes.

24 Reduce the heat to 300°F and cook for another 10–15 minutes, until pale golden brown. Cool slightly before serving.

quiche and pastry variations

Herb Quiche – follow the recipe for Quiche Lorraine but replace the bacon with a large handful of chopped tarragon, chives, parsley and dill.

Onion Quiche – follow the recipe for Quiche Lorraine but replace the bacon with 2 large Spanish onions, finely sliced, and cook in a little oil with a pinch of cayenne pepper until tender and caramelized – this can take up to 45 minutes on a low heat.

Salmon Quiche – follow the recipe for Quiche Lorraine, replacing the bacon with 11 ounces diced cooked salmon and a handful of chopped parsley and tarragon. Omit the cheese but add a pinch of cayenne pepper to the egg mixture.

Zucchini and Spinach Quiche – cook 9 ounces spinach in 3 tablespoons unsalted butter for 2–3 minutes, until wilted, then drain well. Cook 9 ounces sliced zucchini in 3 tablespoons butter for about 5 minutes, until soft, turning frequently, then drain (spinach and zucchini contain a lot of water so it's important to drain them well). Season with salt and pepper and use to replace the Canadian bacon in Quiche Lorraine.

Sweet Pastry – follow the pastry recipe on pages 206–207, omitting the salt and sifting 2.5 ounces confectioner's sugar with the flour.

Polenta Pastry – follow the recipe on pages 206–207, replacing 2.5 ounces of the flour with polenta and stirring in 1 ounce freshly grated Parmesan cheese after rubbing in the butter. Use 2 eggs instead of egg yolks and reduce the water to ½ tablespoon.

TIPS AND IDEAS

■ To get the best results, everything must be cold when making pastry – the butter, the water and your hands. If your hands are warm, you can run them under cold water, but dry thoroughly before making the pastry.

■ The less you handle pastry when making it, the better.

■ If you don't add enough water, the pastry will be too dry and crack during cooking; if you add too much water, it will shrink. The trick is to add enough water so the mixture is not sticky to the touch.

■ Pastry can be made in a food processor, but be sure to use chilled butter and ice-cold water. Put the chilled diced butter and the flour in the processor and blitz until they resemble breadcrumbs. Add the salt (or sugar, if making sweet pastry), followed by the egg yolks and water and process just until the mixture comes together into a ball. Remove, shape into a cylinder, then press down and roll out immediately and use to line your tart pan. Rest it in the fridge before baking.

■ Pastry can be wrapped in plastic wrap and kept in the fridge for 2–3 days; any longer and it tends to turn gray.

■ Both raw and cooked pastry freeze like a dream. You can line a tart pan with it and freeze it in the pan before or after baking blind.

■ When rolling out pastry, always start from the middle, rolling forward and back, then carefully lift the pastry up, give it a quarter turn and start again. You will always find one side of the pastry thicker than the other when you roll it out. Keep turning it regularly, dusting the rolling pin and the work surface lightly with flour as necessary to prevent sticking.

■ When lining a pan with pastry, be careful not to stretch it or it will shrink back during cooking.

■ Resting the pastry in the fridge firms up the butter so the pastry is less likely to shrink in the oven.

■ To use the pastry trimmings, place them on top of each other and press gently together, then roll out.

■ Baking blind may seem like too much trouble but it's worth it – soggy pastry will ruin your dish.

STEAK AND KIDNEY PIE

I'm so happy that dishes like this are coming back into fashion. I was virtually brought up on steak and kidney pie and have fond memories of my mother making it. If you can cook the filling in advance and leave it in the fridge for two days, you will find it tastes even better.

Serves 6

7 ounces ox kidney (or lamb's kidney)

1.5 ounces all-purpose flour

2¼ pounds chuck steak, cut in ¾-inch cubes

olive oil

3 tablespoons unsalted butter

1 large onion, sliced

2 garlic cloves, finely chopped

7 ounces button mushrooms

1 tablespoon thyme leaves

¾ cup red wine

2 cups beef stock (see page 34)

2½ teaspoons Worcestershire sauce

1 quantity of Shortcrust Pastry (see pages 206–207)

1 egg beaten with 1 egg yolk, to glaze

sea salt and black pepper

1 First peel the membrane off the ox kidney and cut the kidney into 3/4-inch pieces. If using lamb's kidney, cut it in half horizontally and remove the tough white cord before cutting into pieces. Put the flour into a large mixing bowl, season with salt and pepper, add the steak and kidney and toss well.

2 Heat some olive oil in a large, heavy-bottomed casserole and brown the floured steak and kidney in it, in batches, over medium heat, making sure you brown the pieces on all sides. Put them in a bowl to one side as you go.

3 When all the meat has been browned, turn the heat down a little, add the butter and cook the onion and garlic until softened. Remove them from the pan and add to the bowl with the beef. Now add the mushrooms and thyme and sauté for 2 minutes. Stir in the leftover flour and cook for a minute longer. Pour in the wine, mix well and return the meat and onion to the pan. Stir in the stock and Worcestershire sauce and bring to the boil.

4 Cover the casserole and transfer to an oven preheated to 350°F. Cook for 1 hour, then reduce the heat to 300°F and cook for another 30 minutes–1 hour, stirring once, until the meat is tender. Remove from the oven and adjust the seasoning. Spoon the meat and a little of the sauce into a 5-cup pie dish, reserving the extra sauce, then leave to cool.

5 Roll out the pastry till it is about 1/8 inch thick and slightly larger than the pie dish. Cut out a strip from it to fit the rim of the dish, brush the rim with water and place the pastry strip on it, pressing it down gently. Brush the pastry rim with egg glaze. If you have a pie funnel (vent), put it in the center of the filling to support the pastry and stop it from sinking into the filling. Lift up the rest of the pastry on your rolling pin and place it on the pie. Trim off the excess pastry with a sharp knife and press the edges of the pie with a fork to seal it firmly. You can cut the trimmings into leaves, if you like, to decorate the top.

6 Brush the top of the pie with beaten egg, then lay any pastry leaves on top and brush them with egg too. Make a hole in the center of the pie, over the funnel if you are using one. Place in an oven preheated to 400°F and bake for 30–40 minutes, until the pastry is golden and crisp. Serve with the extra sauce, reheated.

PORK AND LEEK SAUSAGE ROLLS

These use rough puff pastry, which is a quick alternative to puff pastry.
Light and flaky, it is the perfect casing for sausage rolls.

Makes 8

2 tablespoons unsalted butter

3.5 ounces leeks, finely sliced

1 garlic clove, finely chopped

11 ounces very finely minced pork belly

1 tablespoon chopped sage

1 tablespoon chopped parsley

a pinch of ground mace

1 ounce stale breadcrumbs

sea salt and black pepper

For the rough puff pastry:

9 ounces white bread flour

1 teaspoon salt

6 ounces cold unsalted butter, cut into small cubes

⅔ cup water

1 egg, beaten with 1 egg yolk, to glaze

1 First make the pastry. Sift the flour into a bowl, add the salt and half the butter and rub it into the flour with your fingertips, working as quickly as possible. When the mixture resembles breadcrumbs, add the water, stirring it in with a knife. Use just enough water to gather the dough together. Turn the dough out on to a lightly floured surface and roll it into a rectangle about 1/10 inch thick. Dot half the remaining butter over the bottom two-thirds, then fold the top third down and the bottom third up, like folding a letter. Give the pastry a quarter turn, roll it out again and repeat with the remaining butter. Fold it up in the same way as before, then give it a quarter turn and roll it out again. Fold it up once more, then wrap in plastic wrap and chill for at least 30 minutes.

2 Meanwhile, prepare the filling. Melt the butter in a pan, add the leeks and garlic and cook gently until soft. Leave to cool, then mix with the pork, herbs, mace, breadcrumbs and plenty of salt and pepper. Chill for 30 minutes.

3 Cut the pastry in half and roll each piece into a 4-inch x 12-inch rectangle. Remove the pork mixture from the fridge, divide into two and shape each piece into a long sausage just slightly less than the length of the pastry. Place on the center of each piece of pastry. Brush the edges of the pastry with the egg glaze and fold them over the filling to create a long roll, pressing the edges to seal.

4 Cut each roll into 4. Place seam-side down on a baking sheet, make a couple of slits in the top of each one and brush the top with egg. Place in an oven preheated to 425°F and bake for 10 minutes. Reduce the oven temperature to 350°F and bake for another 15–20 minutes, until golden.

GAME PASTIES

I spent part of my childhood in Cornwall, and consequently I am very fond of pasties. They are delicious but can be quite heavy. These little game pasties make a light alternative to the original and can be served as a starter, canapé or picnic food. They freeze well, but make sure you put them in a hot oven for about 15 minutes before eating.

Makes 15

2 tablespoons unsalted butter

3.5 ounces button mushrooms, finely chopped

14 ounces mixed game, finely minced

7 ounces fatty pork, finely minced

1 teaspoon five-spice powder

2½ tablespoons brandy

2 quantities of Shortcrust Pastry (see pages 206–207)

1 egg beaten with 1 egg yolk, to glaze

sea salt and black pepper

1 Melt the butter in a small frying pan, add the chopped mushrooms and cook over medium heat until they are soft. Season to taste and drain off any juices; it is important to remove most of the moisture from the mushrooms.

2 Put the minced game and pork in a bowl, add the five-spice powder, brandy and mushrooms and season well with salt and pepper. Mix thoroughly, using your hands.

3 Roll out the shortcrust pastry on a lightly floured surface and cut it into 5-inch circles, using a small saucer as a guide and re-rolling the trimmings as necesssary. Place a ball of the filling mixture on each circle, slightly to one side, then brush the pastry edges with the beaten egg. Fold the pastry over and press the edges together to seal, then pinch the sealed edge over repeatedly, turning it inwards, to form a crimp, like a spiral effect.

4 Put the pasties on a baking tray and brush with the remaining beaten egg. Bake in an oven preheated to 350°F for 15–20 minutes, until they are golden brown. Cool slightly before serving.

pasty variations

Chicken Pasties – follow the recipe above, replacing the game with chicken.

Pork and Potato Pasties – omit the game from the recipe above, increase the minced pork to 11 ounces and add 11 ounces diced cooked potatoes.

INDIVIDUAL PEAR AND BLUE CHEESE TARTLETS

I like to use Yorkshire Blue cheese for these little tarts but any good, flavorful blue cheese will work well. If you don't have any individual tart pans, use one 9-inch pan instead and increase the cooking time for the filled tart to about 25 minutes.

Serves 4

1 quantity of Shortcrust Pastry (see pages 206–207)

1 tablespoon unsalted butter

2 ripe pears, peeled, cored and thinly sliced

5 ounces blue cheese, crumbled

3.5 ounces walnuts, lightly toasted in a dry frying pan and then chopped

3½ tablespoons walnut oil

For the onion marmalade:

3 tablespoons unsalted butter

14 ounces onions, finely sliced

2½ tablespoons red wine vinegar

1 tablespoon superfine sugar

sea salt and black pepper

1 First make the onion marmalade. Melt the butter in a non-stick frying pan, add the onions and cook slowly, stirring frequently, until golden and caramelized. This can take up to 1 hour. Add the vinegar, raise the heat and boil for a minute. Add the sugar and mix well. Season to taste and cook for 5 minutes longer, stirring constantly. Remove from the heat and leave to cool.

2 Roll out the pastry on a lightly floured surface to 1/8 inch thick and cut out four 5 1/2-inch circles. Use to line four 4-inch tart pans and bake blind according to the instructions on page 208. Remove the pastry shells from their pans and place carefully (they will be delicate) on a baking tray.

3 Divide the onion marmalade between the pastry cases. Heat the butter in a frying pan, add the pear slices and toss briefly to coat with the butter, then arrange them on top of the onion marmalade. Scatter the cheese over the tartlets, top with the walnuts and drizzle with the walnut oil.

4 Put the tartlets into the oven at 325°F and bake for 15 minutes, until the cheese has melted and is golden brown – if it doesn't brown enough, put under a hot broiler for a few minutes. Serve warm.

TRADITIONAL APPLE PIE

This is a single-crust pie, with pastry on the top rather than top and bottom, meaning you get lots of lovely filling.

Serves 6

2¼ pounds Golden Delicious and Cox's apples, peeled, cored and sliced

3.5 ounces superfine sugar, plus extra for sprinkling

grated zest of 1 lemon

juice and grated zest of 1 orange

1 teaspoon ground cinnamon

1 quantity of Sweet Pastry (see page 210)

1 egg yolk, lightly beaten, to glaze

1 Put the sliced apples into a 5-cup pie dish. Add the sugar, lemon and orange zest, orange juice and cinnamon and mix well.

2 Roll out the pastry till it is about 1/8 inch thick and slightly larger than the pie dish. Cut out a strip from it to fit the rim of the dish, brush the rim with water and place the pastry strip on it, pressing it down gently. Brush the pastry rim with the egg glaze. Lift up the rest of the pastry on your rolling pin and place it on the pie. Trim off the excess pastry with a sharp knife and press the edges of the pie with a fork to seal it firmly. If you like, you can cut out leaves and apples from the pastry trimmings and stick them on top of the pie with the glaze. Sprinkle with a little superfine sugar.

3 Place the pie in an oven preheated to 350°F and bake for 20 minutes, then reduce the heat to 300°F and bake for about 25 minutes longer, until the pastry is golden brown and the apples are tender. Serve with Vanilla Ice Cream (see page 230) or Vanilla Crème Anglaise (see page 226).

Apple pie variation

Apple Crumble – make a crumble by sifting 8 ounces flour into a bowl and rubbing in 5 ounces diced butter with your fingertips until the mixture resembles breadcrumbs. Stir in 2.5 ounces oats, 2 ounces soft brown sugar and 2 ounces superfine sugar. Make the apple filling as above and place in a large pie dish or a gratin dish. Sprinkle the crumble on top and bake at 350°F for 45 minutes, until golden.

MINCE PIES

It's so much nicer to make your own mincemeat, especially as you can put extra booze in it. You'll need to prepare the mincemeat a couple of days in advance.

Makes 30

1½ quantities of Sweet Pastry (see page 210)

1 egg, beaten, to glaze

icing sugar for dusting

For the mincemeat:

4.5 ounces raisins

4.5 ounces golden raisins

4.5 ounces currants

4.5 ounces brown sugar

4.5 ounces suet

2 ounces chopped almonds

2 ounces ginger in syrup, finely chopped

2½ tablespoons brandy

juice and grated zest of 2 oranges

grated zest of 1 lemon

1 large or 2 small Cox's apples, peeled, cored and very finely chopped

1 Put all the ingredients for the mincemeat into a large bowl and mix well. Cover and leave to infuse at room temperature for a couple of days before using.

2 Roll out two-thirds of the pastry on a lightly floured surface to about 1/8 inch thick, then cut out 3-inch circles with a round fluted cutter, re-rolling the trimmings as necessary. Press into the sections of a muffin tin. Put a teaspoonful of mincemeat in each and brush the pastry edges with beaten egg.

3 Roll out the remaining pastry and cut out rounds using a slightly smaller fluted cutter. Place them on top of the mince pies and press the edges together to seal well. Brush with egg and make a couple of tiny slits in each one to allow steam to escape. Place in an oven preheated to 375°F and bake for 20 minutes or until golden brown. Transfer to a wire rack to cool, then serve dusted with confectioner's sugar.

BAKEWELL TART

I like to give Bakewell tart a lattice top, filling the gaps in the lattice with jam, but this is optional and you can omit this stage if you prefer.

Serves 8

1 quantity of Sweet Pastry (see page 210)

1 jar of raspberry jam, warmed and pressed through a sieve

1 egg yolk, to glaze

For the almond cream:

4 eggs

2 egg yolks

4.5 ounces superfine sugar

5 ounces unsalted butter, melted

4.5 ounces ground almonds

1 teaspoon vanilla extract

1 Roll out the pastry to 1/8 inch thick and use to line a 9-inch removable-bottomed tart pan, reserving the pastry trimmings. Bake the pastry shell blind as described on page 208, then leave to cool.

2 To make the almond cream, beat together the eggs, egg yolks and sugar, then mix in the melted butter, ground almonds and vanilla extract.

3 Spread about 7 tablespoons of the raspberry jam over the base of the pastry shell and carefully spread the almond cream on top. Place in an oven preheated to 300°F and bake for about 40 minutes, until the filling is golden and a skewer inserted in the center comes out clean. Remove the tart from the oven and leave to cool completely.

4 If you want to make a lattice, roll out the pastry trimmings very thinly and cut them into strips (or use a lattice cutter). Arrange them on top of the tart in a lattice pattern and brush with the egg glaze, sealing the edges to the rim of the pastry. Place in the oven at 300°F, bake for about 15 minutes, until golden, then remove and leave to cool. Carefully put the rest of the jam in the holes in the lattice.

PLUM FRANGIPANE TART

The secret of a good tart is good pastry, so make sure your pastry is beautifully thin and crisp.

Serves 8

1 quantity of Sweet Pastry (see page 210)

12 ripe plums, halved and pitted

For the frangipane:

3.5 ounces unsalted butter

3.5 ounces confectioner's sugar

3.5 ounces ground almonds

2 eggs

1 ounce all-purpose flour

2½ teaspoons ground cinnamon

1 Roll out the pastry to 1/8 inch thick and use to line a 9-inch removable-bottomed tart pan. Bake it blind as described on page 208, then leave to cool.

2 For the frangipane, beat the butter and confectioner's sugar together until light and fluffy, then mix in the ground almonds, eggs, flour and cinnamon (you can do this in a food processor, if you like).

3 Spread the frangipane over the base of the pastry shell and arrange the halved plums on top, cut-side down, in a neat pattern. Place in an oven preheated to 325°F and bake for about 45 minutes, until the frangipane is set. Allow to cool and serve with cream.

LEMON TART

For the perfect lemon tart, you need the wobble factor. The filling will continue to cook after it comes out of the oven, so a slight wobble means it will have just the right consistency when it has cooled down.

Serves 8

1 quantity of Sweet Pastry (see page 210)

5 medium eggs

1 egg yolk

6 ounces superfine sugar

juice and grated zest of 4 lemons

⅔ cup heavy cream

1 Roll out the pastry to 1/8 inch thick and use to line a 9-inch removable-bottomed tart pan. Bake it blind as described on page 208, then leave to cool.

2 To make the filling, lightly whisk the eggs, the extra yolk and sugar together in a large bowl. Add the lemon juice and zest, followed by the cream, and whisk well to combine. Leave to infuse for about 20 minutes, then strain through a fine sieve.

3 Pour the lemon mixture into the cooled pastry shell, place in an oven preheated to 285°F and bake for 30–35 minutes, until almost, but not quite, set. Allow to cool before serving.

CUSTARDS

Mastering a real egg custard, properly known
as crème anglaise, is a revelation. It is a
joy to make and can be served as a simple
accompaniment to desserts or used as the base of
the most wonderful ice creams. Crème patissière,
or pastry cream, is a truly foolproof form of
custard, because it contains flour, which means
you can boil it without risk of curdling. It is used
for filling tarts and profiteroles and for making
sweet soufflés.

A decent home-made custard is absolutely essential as the base of a classic fruit fool. Mango and passion fruit make a delicious twist on the more traditional gooseberry or rhubarb, and have the advantage that they are available year round and don't need cooking first.

MANGO AND PASSION FRUIT FOOL

To make the basic Crème Anglaise, follow steps 1 to 9

SERVES 6

3 very ripe mangoes

4 ripe passion fruit

½ cup heavy cream

FOR THE CRÈME ANGLAISE:

4 large egg yolks

2.5 ounces superfine sugar

1 cup milk

1 First make the crème anglaise. Put the egg yolks and sugar in a bowl.

2 Whisk the eggs together with a balloon whisk until smooth and slightly paler.

3 Pour the milk into a saucepan and bring to a boil.

4 Remove the milk from the heat and gradually add to the egg mixture, whisking all the time.

5 Return the mixture to the pan; place over a low heat.

6 Stir gently from side to side with a wooden spoon until it begins to thicken. Be careful not to overheat it, as this is when the mixture can curdle.

7 Draw your finger across the back of the custard-coated spoon; if the channel this creates stays clear and does not drip, the custard is ready.

8 Pour the custard through a fine sieve into a bowl and leave to cool.

9 To prevent a skin forming as the custard cools, press a sheet of plastic wrap directly on to the surface.

10 Cut and peel the mangoes, making sure that you get all the flesh off the pit.

11 Cut the passion fruit in half and scoop out the pulp and seeds into a sieve set over a bowl.

12 Push the pulp through the sieve, leaving just the seeds behind (save these to decorate the fool).

13 Put the mango flesh and sieved passion fruit into a food processor and whiz to a purée.

14 Fold the purée into the cold custard.

15 Whip the heavy cream until it forms soft peaks.

16 Then slowly fold the custard into the cream a little at a time.

17 Spoon the fool into individual glasses and chill.

18 Serve the fool topped with the passion fruit seeds.

TIPS AND IDEAS

■ Make crème anglaise in a heavy-bottomed pan, as this distributes the heat evenly.

■ Stir the custard with a wooden spoon, scraping backward and forward over the bottom of the pan in case there are any hot spots. You will eventually feel the mixture start to thicken.

■ If you worry that the custard is overheating, lift it momentarily off the heat and keep stirring.

■ As soon as the custard is done, pour it into a bowl so it stops cooking straight away.

■ If you overcook custard, it will be scrambled and you will have to throw it away. If it is only slightly overcooked (i.e., just beginning to turn grainy), you can often rescue it by pouring it through a fine sieve into a cold bowl, whisking vigorously and then adding a little cream to hold it together.

■ If you are leaving the crème anglaise to cool rather than using it straight away, cover the surface with a piece of plastic wrap to prevent a skin forming.

■ Crème anglaise will keep, covered, in the fridge for 3 days. It is not suitable for freezing, however.

CUSTARDS

crème anglaise variations

Vanilla Crème Anglaise – slit 2 vanilla pods open lengthwise and scrape out the seeds. Follow the recipe on pages 222–223, adding the vanilla seeds to the milk before heating. Alternatively you can add 1 teaspoon of vanilla extract.

Cardamom Crème Anglaise – follow the recipe on pages 222–223, adding 8 lightly crushed cardamom pods to the milk before heating. Bring to a boil and leave to infuse for 30 minutes, then reheat gently and strain before adding to the egg yolk mixture.

Lime Crème Anglaise – follow the recipe on pages 222–223, adding the grated zest of 2 limes to the egg yolk and sugar mixture. Stir the juice of 1 lime into the finished custard but be careful not to thin it too much.

Coffee Crème Anglaise – follow the recipe on pages 222–223, adding 2½ rounded teaspoons of instant coffee to the milk when it comes to a boil.

Grand Marnier Crème Anglaise – follow the recipe on pages 222–223, adding 2½ tablespoons of Grand Marnier to the finished custard.

Chocolate Crème Anglaise – follow the recipe on pages 222–223, adding 2½ tablespoons of cocoa powder to the milk when it comes to a boil.

Ginger Crème Anglaise – finely grate a ¾-inch piece of fresh ginger. Follow the recipe on pages 222–223, adding the ginger to the milk before heating. Leave to infuse for 30 minutes then reheat gently and strain before adding to the egg yolk mixture.

CRÈME BRÛLÉE WITH RASPBERRIES

This makes four very generous portions.

Serves 4

1 vanilla pod

2½ cups heavy cream

7 egg yolks

3 ounces superfine sugar, plus 5 tablespoons for the topping

7 ounces raspberries

1 Slit the vanilla pod open lengthways and scrape out the seeds. Put the cream into a saucepan, add the vanilla seeds and bring to a boil. Remove from the heat and set aside.

2 Put the egg yolks and sugar into a bowl and whisk well, then gradually pour in the cream mixture, whisking all the time. Try not to make too many air bubbles. Strain the mixture through a fine sieve.

3 Divide the raspberries between 4 round, eared dishes (3/4–1 cup in capacity), arranging them so they stand upright. Pour on the custard mixture. Put the dishes on to a tray and bake in an oven preheated to 285°F for 25 minutes or until the custard is just set. Remove and allow to cool, then chill.

4 Sprinkle a tablespoon of superfine sugar evenly over each crème brûlée and then caramelize with a kitchen blowtorch, keeping it moving and being careful not to burn the sugar (if you don't have a blowtorch, you can put the crème brûlées under a very hot broiler to caramelize, but a blowtorch works best). Leave them to cool and then serve.

RHUBARB TRIFLE WITH GINGER BEER JELLY

This dish is well worth making when rhubarb is in season. You need to use a ginger beer with a good flavor. There will be some sponge left over but you can freeze it for another occasion.

Serves 4–6

1 quantity of Crème Anglaise (see pages 222–223)

a little raspberry eau-de-vie for sprinkling

For the sponge:

5 ounces ground almonds

6 ounces superfine sugar

3 eggs

2 ounces all-purpose flour

2 tablespoons unsalted butter, melted

½ teaspoon vanilla extract

3 egg whites

For the ginger jelly:

3 gelatin sheets

1¼ cups ginger beer

⅛ cup water

2.5 ounces superfine sugar

For the rhubarb compote:

18 ounces rhubarb, cut into ¾-inch lengths

3.5 ounces superfine sugar

¼ cup orange juice

3½ tablespoons water

1 First make the sponge. Put the almonds, 5 ounces of the superfine sugar, the eggs, flour, melted butter and vanilla extract into a large bowl and whisk until combined. In a large, clean bowl, whisk the egg whites with the remaining superfine sugar until stiff. Fold them into the cake mixture, then put it on a baking sheet lined with baking parchment and spread it out in a layer about 1/4 inch thick. Place in an oven preheated to 350°F and bake for 12–15 minutes, until golden brown. Leave to cool, then invert the sponge onto a work surface and peel off the paper.

2 To make the ginger jelly, soak the gelatin sheets in a large, shallow dish of cold water for 10–15 minutes, until soft. Pour the ginger beer into a glass bowl and whisk to get rid of the carbonation. It should be totally flat. Heat the ginger beer gently in a pan with the water, add the sugar and stir until dissolved. Remove from the heat. Drain the gelatin sheets, gently squeeze out excess water, then add them to the pan and stir until completely melted. Leave the jelly in the fridge for about half an hour, until just before it starts to set.

3 For the compote, put the rhubarb into a saucepan, add the sugar, orange juice and water and bring to a boil. Simmer gently for 4–5 minutes, until tender, then remove from the heat and strain the juice into another saucepan. Boil until reduced to about 5 tablespoons, then stir the rhubarb back in and leave to cool.

4 To assemble the trifle, cut the sponge into pieces to fit 4–6 glasses (or use one large bowl, if you prefer) and sprinkle them with eau-de-vie. Put a layer of sponge in each glass, top with some rhubarb compote, then add another layer of sponge, then some ginger beer jelly. Put the trifle into the fridge so the jelly sets. Top with the crème anglaise and serve.

BREAD AND BUTTER PUDDING

Serves 4–6

1 ounce golden raisins

2½ tablespoons rum

8 large slices of brioche or white bread

4 tablespoons unsalted butter

For the custard:

2 vanilla pods

4 large eggs

2 egg yolks

3.5 ounces superfine sugar, plus extra for dusting

1⅔ cups heavy cream

½ cup whole milk

1 rounded teaspoon ground cinnamon

1 Put the golden raisins in a small bowl, pour the rum over and leave to soak for a couple of hours.

2 Cut the crusts off the brioche or bread, butter each piece generously and then cut in half on the diagonal. Generously butter a 4 1/2-cup gratin dish, about 10 x 7 inches, then overlap the triangles of bread in the dish in rows, with the points sticking up.

3 To make the custard, slit the vanilla pods open lengthways and scrape out the seeds. Put the eggs and egg yolks into a bowl, add the sugar and the vanilla seeds and whisk well. Put the cream, milk and cinnamon in a saucepan, bring to a boil, then gradually pour on to the egg mixture, whisking well. Strain through a fine sieve. Pour the custard over the bread and sprinkle on the golden raisins and any remaining rum. Gently push the bread down to submerge it, then leave the pudding to stand for 45 minutes.

4 Put the dish in a roasting pan and pour enough hot water into the pan to come about halfway up the sides of the dish. Place in an oven preheated to 350°F and bake for 30–40 minutes, until just firm to the touch. Remove the pudding from the oven and leave to cool for 30 minutes before serving. If you like, you could sprinkle on some sugar and caramelize the top with a blowtorch or under a very hot broiler.

BLUEBERRY TART WITH CRÈME PATISSIÈRE

This tart is delicious with blueberries but it also works very well with other soft fruits, such as raspberries, strawberries, figs or sliced peaches.

Serves 4

1 quantity of Sweet Pastry (see page 210)

⅔ cup heavy cream

18 ounces blueberries

confectioner's sugar for dusting

For the crème patissière:

4 egg yolks

1 ounce all-purpose flour

1 teaspoon cornstarch

2.5 ounces superfine sugar

1¼ cups whole milk

1 Roll out the pastry to 1/8 inch thick and use to line a 9-inch removable-bottomed tart pan. Bake it blind as described on page 208, then leave to cool.

2 To make the crème pâtissière, put the egg yolks, flour, cornstarch and sugar in a bowl and whisk with a balloon whisk to combine. Bring the milk to a boil in a saucepan, then remove from the heat and pour on to the egg mixture, whisking all the time. Return the mixture to the pan and heat slowly, stirring constantly, until it starts to thicken. Continue to cook for 1–2 minutes, stirring all the time. Remove from the heat and push through a sieve into a bowl. Cover with plastic wrap and leave to cool completely.

3 Whip the cream to very soft peaks and fold it into the crème pâtissière. Fill the pastry shell to about 1/2 inch from the top with this mixture and level it with a spatula. Top with the blueberries and dust with confectioner's sugar.

CUSTARD TARTS
WITH CINNAMON

Serves 14

1 cup heavy cream

1 cup whipping cream

2 cinnamon sticks

4 egg yolks

5 ounces superfine sugar

a few drops of vanilla extract

1.5 ounces cornstarch

14 ounces puff pastry

1 Put the heavy and whipping cream in a saucepan with the cinnamon sticks and bring to a simmer. Turn the heat off and leave for at least an hour in order to infuse the cream with the cinnamon.

2 Put the egg yolks, sugar, vanilla extract and cornstarch in a large bowl and beat until smooth. Gradually stir in the infused cream, discarding the cinnamon sticks. Pour into a clean pan and slowly bring to a simmer, stirring constantly, until the custard has thickened. Remove from the heat and leave to cool completely.

3 Roll the puff pastry out on a lightly floured surface to 1/4 inch thick. Roll it up into a tight, long sausage and cut it into 14 pieces. Take one piece and place it flat-side down, then roll it out again quite thinly. Repeat with the remaining pieces of pastry.

4 Butter 14 muffin cups and line them with the pieces of pastry, making sure they are well pressed down into the edges of the cups. Spoon in the custard and place in an oven preheated to 350°F. Bake for about 20 minutes, until the pastry is golden. Remove from the oven and leave to cool.

VANILLA ICE CREAM

This is the base for all kinds of ice creams (see opposite) but don't forget how delicious it is on its own.

Serves 4

2 quantities of Vanilla Crème Anglaise (see page 226)

¼ cup heavy cream

1 Put the cold crème anglaise into an ice cream machine and churn for about 20 minutes. Add the cream and continue churning until mixed in and softly frozen (the reason for adding the cream later is so it stays creamy and doesn't crystallize). Transfer to a freezer container and freeze until required. I like to take it out of the freezer about 10 minutes before serving, so it can soften slightly.

2 If you don't have an ice cream machine, pour the mixture into a shallow container and freeze for about an hour, until it is firm around the edges. Remove from the freezer and whisk well to get rid of ice crystals, then return to the freezer. Repeat a couple of times, then freeze until solid.

ice cream variations

Honey Ice Cream – follow the recipe for Vanilla Ice Cream, reducing the number of vanilla pods to 2 and stirring 3½ tablespoons of honey into the custard before leaving it to cool. I like to use acacia honey.

Blackberry Ice Cream – gently cook 1 pound blackberries with 2½ tablespoons of superfine sugar until soft, then push them through a fine sieve to remove the seeds and leave to cool. Make 1 quantity of Crème Anglaise (see pages 222–223). Add the blackberry purée to the cooled custard and stir in the juice of ½ lemon, or to taste. Freeze as for Vanilla Ice Cream, adding ¼ cup heavy cream after churning for 20 minutes.

Lemon Mascarpone Ice Cream – put the juice and grated zest of 3–4 lemons (you need ½ cup juice) in a pan with 4 ounces superfine sugar and bring to a boil, stirring to dissolve the sugar. Make 1 quantity of Crème Anglaise (see pages 222–223), replacing the milk with the lemon mixture and ½ cup whole milk. Leave to cool completely. Put 9 ounces mascarpone cheese and ¼ cup heavy cream in a bowl and beat with a fork until smooth. Add to the cooled lemon crème anglaise. Freeze as for Vanilla Ice Cream, above.

Coconut and Ginger Ice Cream – make 2 quantities of Crème Anglaise (see pages 222–223), using half whole milk and half coconut milk instead of milk. Freeze as for Vanilla Ice Cream, stirring in ⅛ cup rum and 2–3 pieces of candied stem ginger, finely chopped, with the ¼ cup heavy cream.

Chocolate and Hazelnut Ice Cream – toast 5 ounces hazelnuts in an oven preheated to 350°F until lightly colored, then tip them into a tea towel and rub them together to remove the skins. Put the nuts in a food processor with 1.5 ounces cocoa powder and process to a paste. Make 2 quantities of Crème Anglaise (see pages 222–223), adding an extra 3.5 ounces superfine sugar to the egg yolks. Cool the custard slightly, then gradually stir in the hazelnut paste until smooth. Freeze as for Vanilla Ice Cream, using ½ cup heavy cream instead of ¼ cup.

Coffee Ice Cream – make 2 quantities of Crème Anglaise (see pages 222–223), adding 2½ rounded tablespoons of instant coffee to the milk before heating. Freeze as for Vanilla Ice Cream.

MERINGUES

I always end up with loads of egg whites after making mayonnaise, hollandaise and custards and the most obvious thing to do with them is to make meringues. In my experience, everyone adores them, and although many of them need a fairly long cooking time they are very quick to whip up.

*A pavlova is a dramatic dessert that really makes a statement.
One of the lovely things about it is that you can decorate it
with any seasonal fruit. It is one of the easiest meringues to
make, because you don't need to worry too much about shaping
it perfectly.*

RASPBERRY PAVLOVA

To make the basic Meringue mixture, follow steps 1 to 6

SERVES 8

1½ cups heavy cream

1 ounce confectioner's sugar

14 ounces raspberries

FOR THE MERINGUE:

4 egg whites, at room temperature

4 ounces superfine sugar

4 ounces confectioner's sugar

1 teaspoon white wine vinegar

1 teaspoon cornstarch

2 drops of vanilla extract

1 First make the meringue. Put the egg whites into a large bowl and whisk with an electric beater until they form soft peaks.

2 Gradually add the superfine sugar and keep whisking until the meringue stiffens.

3 Sift in the confectioner's sugar.

4 Whisk until incorporated.

5 Mix the vinegar, cornstarch and vanilla extract in a small bowl.

6 Add to the meringue mixture and fold it in with a large metal spoon.

7 Line a baking sheet with a piece of baking parchment and draw a circle on the paper about 8 inches in diameter – you could draw around a cake pan.

8 Spoon the meringue onto the circle. Flatten it slightly or leave it rough. Put into an oven preheated to 225°F and bake for 2½ hours.

9 Turn off the oven and leave the meringue in it for another hour to cool. Remove from the oven.

10 Carefully peel the paper off the base and leave to cool completely.

11 Put the heavy cream in a large bowl.

12 Sift in the confectioner's sugar.

13 Whip until the cream forms soft peaks.

14 Gently spread the cream over the meringue.

15 Then top with the raspberries.

TIPS AND IDEAS

■ Make sure the bowl in which you whisk the egg whites is spotlessly clean, otherwise they will not whip up properly. Any speck of yolk in the whites will also have this effect, so be careful not to break the yolks when separating the eggs.

■ Don't over beat the egg whites before you add the superfine sugar, just take them to soft peaks – otherwise they can separate and become grainy. After adding the sugar, you can whisk the mixture for about 4 minutes with an electric beater, longer by hand if necessary.

■ You could cook the meringue on a silicone baking mat instead of baking parchment, if you like – just place a large ring on the mat to shape the meringue.

■ Meringues can expand during cooking, so remember this when you are shaping your uncooked meringue.

■ The oven temperature should be very low so the meringue doesn't color.

■ Leaving the meringue to cool in the turned-off oven helps to prevent it cracking.

■ Pavlova has a soft, marshmallowy texture – a result of adding the vinegar and cornstarch. If you would like a crisper pavlova, use the Classic Meringue mixture (see page 240) instead.

pavlova variations

Exotic Fruit Pavlova – follow the recipe on pages 234–236, replacing the raspberries with 2 mangoes, peeled and diced, and the seeds and juice from 6 ripe passion fruit.

Hazelnut Pavlova – follow the recipe on pages 234–236, substituting soft light brown sugar for the confectioner's sugar and folding in 2 ounces ground hazelnuts with the cornstarch mixture.

Chocolate and Raspberry Pavlova – follow the recipe on pages 234–236, drizzling 5 ounces melted dark chocolate over the cooled pavlova base and allowing it to set before topping with the cream and raspberries.

Fig and Honey Pavlova – make the pavlova base, following the recipe on on pages 234–236), and then whip the heavy cream without the sugar, folding 3½ tablespoons of runny honey into the whipped cream instead. Substitute 10 very ripe figs, cut into eighths, for the raspberries. Scatter with toasted slivered almonds and then swirl a tablespoon of honey mixed with a teaspoon of Vin Santo or another sweet white wine all over the finished pavlova.

STRAWBERRY MERINGUE ROULADE

This sounds scary but it's incredibly easy to do. You've got to keep the roulade tight when you roll it and lift it as you roll, so it is as round as possible.

Serves 6

6 egg whites

12 ounces superfine sugar

2½ tablespoons cornstarch

2½ teaspoons cider vinegar

a handful of sliced almonds, to decorate

For the filling:

1½ cups heavy cream

2 ounces confectioner's sugar

11 ounces strawberries, sliced

1 Put the egg whites into a large bowl and whisk with an electric beater until they form soft peaks. Add half the sugar and continue whisking for 5 minutes, until the mixture is very stiff. Whisk in the cornstarch and cider vinegar, then whisk in the other half of the sugar.

2 Line a baking sheet with baking parchment, then put the meringue on top, spreading it out into a rectangle about 1/2 inch thick. Place in an oven preheated to 270°F and bake for about 25 minutes, until the meringue is pale golden.

3 For the filling, whip the heavy cream with the confectioner's sugar until quite stiff and keep it in the fridge until ready to use.

4 Remove the meringue from the oven and leave to cool. Lay a clean tea towel on a work surface, turn the meringue upside down on to it and carefully peel off the baking parchment. Spread the whipped cream all over the meringue and top with the sliced strawberries. Now lift the cloth and use it to help you roll up the roulade. You can keep it in the fridge for several hours, or even overnight, at this stage. When you are ready to serve, carefully transfer the roulade to a plate and decorate it with the sliced almonds.

BAKED ALASKA

The exciting thing about this is that you have hot meringue coming out of the oven with still-frozen ice cream hidden inside. It never fails to thrill.

Serves 6

1 quantity of Vanilla Ice Cream (see page 230)

1 sponge cake (use the trifle sponge on page 227)

3½ tablespoons strawberry jam, warmed and pressed through a sieve

4 egg whites

4 ounces superfine sugar

4 ounces confectioner's sugar, sifted

1 Take a 5-cup ovenproof bowl and line it with a double layer of plastic wrap. Fill the bowl with the ice cream, then turn it out of the bowl on to a tray lined with baking parchment and put it into the freezer. Leave it there for at least 2 hours.

2 Cut the sponge into a round slightly larger than the top of the bowl. Spread the strawberry jam over the sponge, top with the ice cream and put it back into the freezer on the parchment-lined tray.

3 Shortly before you wish to serve, put the egg whites into a large bowl and whisk with an electric beater until they form fairly stiff peaks. Add the superfine sugar and whisk for about 5 minutes, until stiff, then fold in the confectioner's sugar with a large metal spoon.

4 Remove the ice cream from the freezer and use a spatula to cover it with the meringue, making sure the ice cream and sponge are entirely covered and there are no gaps. If you prefer, you can pipe it on using a star nozzle. Place in an oven preheated to 450°F and bake for 3–4 minutes, until golden brown. Serve immediately.

TINY MERINGUE MOUTHFULS

These are very quick to make and take only about 15 minutes to cook. They are a little sweeter than the classic meringue.

Makes about 50

4 egg whites

7 ounces superfine sugar

6 ounces confectioner's sugar, sifted

2.5 ounces slivered almonds

cocoa powder for dusting (optional)

1 Put the egg whites into a large bowl and whisk with an electric beater until they form soft peaks. Add the superfine sugar and beat for about 5 minutes, until stiff. Fold in the confectioner's sugar with a large metal spoon and then fold in the almonds.

2 Put rounded teaspoonfuls of the meringue onto a large baking sheet lined with baking parchment. Place in an oven preheated to 300°F and bake for 15 minutes, until crisp on the outside but still soft and marshmallowy inside – they might need a couple more minutes. Remove from the baking parchment with a spatula and leave to cool. Dust with cocoa powder before serving, if you like.

Classic meringue variations

Chocolate Meringues – break up 5 ounces dark chocolate and put it in a bowl set over a pan of gently simmering water, making sure the water isn't touching the base of the bowl. Dip about a third of each meringue into the chocolate and leave on a sheet of baking parchment until set. Sandwich together with whipped cream as opposite.

Meringue Nests – make the Classic Meringue mixture opposite, then put it in a piping bag fitted with a ½-inch plain or star nozzle. Line a baking sheet with baking parchment and pipe 3-inch rings on the paper. Pipe thinly inside each ring to make a base, then pipe another couple of layers on top of the edge to create a wall. Bake as opposite. Serve filled with whipped cream or ice cream and topped with fruit.

Eton Mess – this is a wonderful way of using up leftover meringues. I haven't given quantities here, because you can just use whatever you have. Break the meringues into small chunks and fold them into plenty of whipped cream with some quartered strawberries. You can drizzle some strawberry purée on top, if you like, or fold it in to create a ripple effect.

CLASSIC MERINGUES

The fun thing about meringues is that you can make them into any shape you like. Hearts look lovely. But remember that when you cook them they always get a little bigger. Meringues will keep for ages in an airtight tin.

Makes 12

4 egg whites

4 ounces superfine sugar

a pinch of salt

1 teaspoon lemon juice

4 ounces confectioner's sugar, sifted

For the filling:

1¼ cups heavy cream

3½ tablespoons confectioner's sugar

1 Put the egg whites into a large bowl and whisk with an electric beater until they form soft peaks. Add the superfine sugar and salt and continue to whisk until the egg whites are very stiff. Whisk in the lemon juice, then fold in the confectioner's sugar with a large metal spoon.

2 Take a tablespoonful of the mixture, push it along the side of the bowl to give a good shape and then turn it off the spoon onto a parchment-lined baking sheet. Repeat with the remaining mixture. Place in an oven preheated to 200°F and bake for 1 1/2 hours. Turn the oven off and leave the meringues in it until cold.

3 For the filling, pour the cream into a bowl, sift in the confectioner's sugar and whip until the cream forms firm peaks. Use to sandwich the meringues together.

CAKES

I can honestly say that some of my best
memories are of making cakes with my children
and grandchildren. It's a wonderful way to
communicate with them. Cakes are very simple
and need few ingredients, mainly cupboard items.
The wonderful aroma filling the kitchen, the
laughter and excitement, licking out the bowl, the
anticipation as it bakes, then, best of all, eating
it — what could be nicer?

This is a very simple cake to start off with, and in my opinion one of the greatest. Once you have mastered this cake, you have the base for all sorts of variations. See page 248 for some suggestions to get you started.

VICTORIA SPONGE CAKE

8 ounces soft unsalted butter, plus extra for greasing

8 ounces superfine sugar

4 large eggs

8 ounces self-rising flour

7 tablespoons raspberry jam

1–2½ tablespoons confectioner's sugar

1 First prepare two 8-inch cake pans by greasing them well with butter.

2 Line the base of each pan with a circle of baking parchment cut to fit.

3 Put the soft butter and the sugar in a large mixing bowl.

4 Beat the butter and sugar together until fluffy and almost white in color. This is easiest with an electric beater but you can also use a wooden spoon.

5 Lightly whisk the eggs together in a small glass or bowl.

6 Add to the butter mixture a little at a time, beating constantly.

7 Now sift in the flour in 3 or 4 additions.

8 Fold in the flour each time with a large metal spoon. Be careful not to knock the air out or the cake will be heavy.

9 Divide the cake mixture equally between the 2 cake pans and level the surface.

10 Place on the middle rack of an oven preheated to 350°F and bake for 25–30 minutes, until well risen and golden brown.

11 To check if the cakes are done, press one gently in the middle with your finger – it should spring back up.

12 If you're still not sure, insert a skewer in the center – if it comes out clean, the cake is cooked through.

13 Remove the cakes from the oven and leave in the pans for 10 minutes. Then run a knife around the edge of each one to loosen it if necessary.

14 Turn out the cakes onto a wire rack. Leave to cool completely.

15 Peel off the baking parchment and put one of the cakes on a serving plate.

16 Spread the raspberry jam over the top of the cake.

17 Put the other cake on top of the jam.

18 Then sift the confectioner's sugar over the top through a fine sieve.

TIPS AND IDEAS

■ Greasing and lining the cake pan before baking not only prevents the cake sticking; it also gives it a softer exterior.

■ Beat in the eggs a little at a time to try to prevent curdling. Don't worry too much if the mixture does curdle though, because as soon as the flour is added it will bring it back together. The texture will be slightly denser but the cake will be fine.

■ Sift the flour directly on to the mixture and fold it in carefully so you don't knock out all the air you have beaten in. To fold, use a large metal spoon (a metal spoon cuts through better than a wooden spoon) and get it under the mixture, turning it over rather than stirring it; go round the sides and through the middle as gently as possible until all the flour is mixed in.

■ You don't have to stick to a round cake pan: you can use a square or oblong tin or even cook the cake in a Pyrex dish. Do be sure to use the right size, however. A 7-inch square cake pan roughly equals an 8-inch round one. If you want to use a bigger pan, use one and a half times the quantity of the mixture, or even double it, remembering that it will take a little longer to cook.

■ During baking, things can happen to cakes, but don't worry – it's usually something that's simple to correct next time. Sometimes they crack or have a peak in the middle, which means the oven was too hot. If they sink, the oven was too cool or you haven't beaten the mixture enough.

■ If you want to frost a cake and the top has peaked slightly, you can always trim it and then turn it over.

■ When storing cakes, I always line the pans with wax paper to protect them. Most cakes keep well in an airtight container – up to a week for a Victoria sponge. The higher the fat content, the better they will keep. Sponge cakes freeze well without their fillings.

■ Leftover stale sponge can be used to make trifles (see page 227).

victoria sponge variations

Lemon or Orange Sponge Cake – follow the recipe on pages 244–246, adding the zest of 2 lemons or oranges to the butter and sugar mixture. Sandwich together with lemon or orange butter cream (see below).

Chocolate Cake – follow the recipe on pages 244–246, taking out 2½ level tablespoons of the flour and replacing it with the same amount of cocoa powder. Fill the cake with a chocolate ganache, made by bringing ¾ cup heavy cream to a boil, then removing from the heat and adding 7 ounces finely chopped plain chocolate (60 percent cocoa solids). Leave to stand for 5 minutes, then stir gently to make a smooth cream. Cool slightly and stir in 1½ tablespoons soft butter. Cool completely before using.

Coffee Cake – mix 1 tablespoon of instant coffee with 2½ teaspoons of boiling water to make a smooth paste. Follow the recipe on pages 244–246, adding the coffee mixture to the whisked eggs. Sandwich together with coffee butter cream (see below).

Jam and Cream Sponge Cake – whip ⅔ cup heavy cream with 2½ tablespoons of confectioner's sugar until it forms soft peaks. Fill the Victoria sponge cake with the jam, spreading the whipped cream over the jam.

Victoria Sponge Cake with Fresh Berries – beat 5 ounces mascarpone cheese with 2½ tablespoons of confectioner's sugar to make a soft cream. Spread over the bottom half of the cake and top with 9 ounces berries, sliced if large. Top with the other half of the cake and dust with confectioner's sugar.

Butter cream filling – beat 6 tablespoons soft unsalted butter until very pale and fluffy, then gradually beat in 5 ounces sifted confectioner's sugar, followed by 2½ tablespoons of heavy cream. For lemon or orange butter cream, beat in the grated zest of 1 lemon or orange plus 1 tablespoon of the juice. For coffee butter cream, beat in 2½ tablespoons of very strong black coffee. For vanilla butter cream, beat in a few drops of vanilla extract.

Fairy Cakes – make half the Victoria Sponge Cake mixture and divide between 12–16 small paper cupcake liners, filling them two-thirds full. Bake at 350°F for 15–20 minutes, until risen and golden. Leave to cool, then decorate with a glacé icing made by gradually stirring 1–2½ tablespoons of lemon juice or warm water into 4–6 ounces sifted confectioner's sugar; the icing should be thick enough to coat the back of a spoon.

Lemon Drizzle Cake – follow the recipe on pages 244–246, adding the grated zest of 2 lemons to the eggs, then slowly adding the juice of the lemons to them. Bake in a greased and lined deep 9-inch cake pan for 40–45 minutes. Meanwhile, slowly heat 5 ounces superfine sugar in a pan with 2 cups water and the zest of 2 lemons, pared off in strips with a vegetable peeler (without the white pith). Simmer for about 15 minutes, until it has reduced by half, then leave to cool and remove the peel. When you take the cake out of the oven, make holes all over it with a skewer and slowly pour on the lemon syrup, so it is absorbed by the cake. Leave to cool in the pan.

PLUM UPSIDE-DOWN CAKE

Here, the basic Victoria sponge mixture is used to make a simple pudding cake. Other fruits work well too — try blackberries, apples, pears or apricots.

8 ounces soft unsalted butter, plus extra for greasing

8 ounces superfine sugar

4 large eggs

a few drops of vanilla extract

8 ounces all-purpose flour

2½ rounded teaspoons baking powder

5 ounces ground almonds

8–10 plums, depending on size, halved and pitted

1 Grease a deep 10-inch round cake pan with butter and line the base with baking parchment.

2 Put the butter and the sugar in a large mixing bowl and beat together until fluffy and almost white in color. Lightly whisk the eggs together and add to the butter mixture a little at a time, beating constantly. Mix in the vanilla extract. Sift in the flour and baking powder in 3 or 4 additions, folding them in with a large metal spoon. Finally, fold in the ground almonds.

3 Arrange the plums skin-side up in the base of the cake pan. Spoon the cake mixture on top, smooth the surface, then put the cake into an oven preheated to 300°F. Bake for about 1 hour and 20 minutes, until the cake is well risen and golden and a skewer inserted in the center comes out clean. Leave it in the pan for 30 minutes before turning out. Serve warm as a pudding, with cream or ice cream, or cold, as a cake with coffee or tea.

ULTIMATE CHOCOLATE CAKE

This is a very rich chocolate cake but not at all cloying. Dark and elegant, it doesn't need any embellishment, except perhaps a dusting of confectioner's sugar if you fancy it. Serve with Vanilla Ice Cream (see page 230).

8 ounces unsalted butter, diced, plus extra for greasing

8 ounces plain chocolate

4 eggs, separated

8 ounces superfine sugar

3.5 ounces self-rising flour

1 Grease a 10-inch round cake pan with butter and line the base with baking parchment.

2 Break up the chocolate and put it in a heatproof bowl with the butter. Place the bowl over a pan of gently simmering water, making sure the water doesn't touch the base of the bowl, and leave until the chocolate has melted.

3 Put the egg yolks in a large bowl, add the sugar and beat until pale and fluffy. Gently mix in the melted chocolate. Sift in the flour and fold it in with a large metal spoon.

4 In a separate bowl, beat the egg whites until they form stiff peaks. Fold them into the chocolate mixture and then pour into the prepared pan. Place in an oven preheated to 350°F and bake for about 45 minutes, until the cake is firm to the touch and a skewer inserted in the center comes out clean. Leave the cake to cool in the pan for about 15 minutes, then turn out on to a wire rack to cool completely.

CIAMBELLA

Ciambella is an Italian ring cake. You can serve it with the central hole filled with fresh berries, which looks wonderful. The cake mixture is very firm but don't worry – this is how it is meant to be.

3.5 ounces unsalted butter

11 ounces all-purpose flour, plus extra for dusting

3 teaspoons cream of tartar

1 teaspoon baking soda

6 ounces superfine sugar

2 eggs

grated zest of 1 orange (use a Seville orange if they are in season)

grated zest of 1 lemon

5 tablespoons sweet white wine

1 Melt the butter over a low heat, then use a little of it to brush the inside of an 8 1/2-inch Bundt pan. Dust the pan with flour, tipping out any excess.

2 Sift the flour, cream of tartar and baking soda into a large bowl. Add the remaining melted butter and the superfine sugar and mix well.

3 In a separate bowl, whisk the eggs together until pale. Whisk in the orange and lemon zest and the wine, then add to the flour mixture and beat well. Spoon the mixture into the prepared pan and place in an oven preheated to 375°F. Bake for 30 minutes or until a skewer inserted in the center comes out clean. Leave the cake in the pan for 10 minutes, then turn out on to a wire rack and leave to cool completely.

CHOCOLATE AND WALNUT BROWNIES

Makes 20

6 ounces dark chocolate

6 ounces unsalted butter, diced

3 eggs

9 ounces superfine sugar

1½ teaspoons vanilla extract

4 ounces all-purpose flour

a pinch of salt

½ teaspoon baking powder

5 ounces walnuts, roughly chopped

1 Break up the chocolate and put it in a bowl with the diced butter. Place the bowl over a pan of gently simmering water, making sure the water does not touch the base of the bowl. Leave until melted.

2 Put the eggs, sugar and vanilla extract in a large bowl and whisk until pale. Gently mix the melted chocolate into the egg mixture. Sift in the flour, salt and baking powder and then fold them in gently. Finally, add the walnuts.

3 Transfer the mixture to a parchment-lined baking pan about 8 1/2 inches square. Bake in an oven preheated to 325°F for 25–30 minutes, or until firm to the touch. Be careful not to overcook the brownies – a skewer inserted in the center should come out with just a little of the mixture adhering to it. Leave to cool, then cut into squares to serve.

APPLE AND PEAR CAKE

I like to serve this warm, with whipped cream or ice cream, as a lunchtime dessert.

5 tablespoons unsalted butter, plus extra for greasing

5 ounces superfine sugar

2 eggs, lightly beaten

4 ounces all-purpose flour

4 ounces self-rising flour

½ teaspoon baking soda

1 teaspoon cream of tartar

½ teaspoon ground cinnamon

2½ tablespoons apple juice

2 tart apples, preferably Granny Smiths, peeled, cored and cut into small dice

2 pears, peeled, cored and cut into small dice

2½ tablespoons pine nuts

1 tablespoon granulated sugar

1 Grease a 9-inch cake pan and line the base and sides with baking parchment. Using a wooden spoon or an electric beater, beat the butter and sugar together in a bowl until light and fluffy. Beat in the eggs a little at a time.

2 Sift in the flours, baking soda, cream of tartar and cinnamon and fold them in with a large metal spoon. Fold in the apple juice and then the diced fruit.

3 Transfer the mixture to the prepared cake pan, smooth the top and sprinkle with the pine nuts and granulated sugar. Place in an oven preheated to 325°F and bake for about 1 hour, until the cake is well risen and a skewer inserted in the center comes out clean. Turn out on to a wire rack and leave to cool.

RUM AND FRUIT LOAF

This simple tea bread is given a bit of a kick by the rum. It keeps well and is very good sliced and buttered.

5 tablespoons unsalted butter, plus extra for greasing

2.5 ounces superfine sugar

1 pound mixed dried fruit

1 ounce sliced almonds

1 large egg, lightly beaten

⅛ cup strong black tea, left to cool

2½ tablespoons rum

2.5 ounces self-rising flour

2.5 ounces all-purpose flour

½ teaspoon ground pie spice

½ teaspoon baking soda

1 Grease a 7 x 4 1/2 x 3 inch loaf pan with butter and line the base with baking parchment.

2 Melt the butter and sugar in a large saucepan. Remove from the heat, stir in the dried fruit and almonds, then transfer to a large bowl. Stir in the egg, followed by the tea and rum. Sift in the flours, pie spice and baking soda and mix well.

3 Transfer the mixture to the loaf pan and place in an oven preheated to 300°F. Bake for 1–1 1/2 hours, until the loaf is firm to the touch and a skewer inserted in the center comes out clean. Remove the loaf from the oven and leave to cool for an hour before turning it out on to a wire rack to cool completely. Wrap in foil and store overnight before slicing.

STICKY TOFFEE PUDDINGS

This is everybody's favorite pudding and I think it's something everyone should make. If you want to steam the puddings, simply put the foil-covered bowls into a steamer and cook for 40 minutes. You can also bake the sponge, uncovered, in an 8-inch square pan for about 40 minutes and cut it into squares to serve.

Serves 6

6 tablespoons softened unsalted butter, plus extra for greasing

7 ounces dates, Medjool if possible, pitted and chopped (or 6 ounces ready-pitted dates, chopped)

1¼ cups water

1 teaspoon baking soda

6 ounces soft dark brown sugar

2 eggs

a few drops of vanilla extract

6 ounces self-rising flour

For the toffee sauce:

5 ounces butter

5 ounces light muscovado sugar

¾ cup heavy cream

1 Butter 6 individual ovenproof bowls or metal molds, about 3/4 cup in capacity.

2 Put the dates and water into a small saucepan, bring to a boil and simmer to a thickened, gooey mass. This will take at least 15 minutes. Stir in the baking soda and leave to cool.

3 Beat the butter and sugar together until paler in color, then beat in the eggs one at a time, followed by the vanilla extract. Sift in the flour and fold it in with a large metal spoon. Finally fold in the cooked date mixture.

4 Divide the mixture between the bowls or molds, then cover each with a piece of buttered foil, making a pleat in the center of the foil to allow the puddings to rise. Place in an oven preheated to 350°F and bake for 20–25 minutes, until the puddings are well risen and a skewer inserted in the center comes out clean.

5 While the puddings are in the oven, make the toffee sauce: put the butter and sugar in a small saucepan and heat gently, stirring to dissolve the sugar. Pour in the heavy cream, raise the heat and let it bubble for 5–10 minutes, until the sauce has thickened a little and turned a slightly darker caramel color.

6 When the puddings are done, turn them out onto individual plates and cover with the toffee sauce. Serve immediately, with Vanilla Ice Cream (see page 230) or cream.

CHOCOLATE ROULADE WITH CHERRIES

This is a fairly elaborate but very useful dessert, as you can make it well in advance and keep it in the fridge until you are ready to serve.

6 ounces plain chocolate

6 eggs, separated

6 ounces superfine sugar

cocoa powder for dusting

7 ounces black cherries in kirsch, drained

⅔ cup heavy cream

1 ounce confectioner's sugar, plus extra for dusting

For the chocolate ganache filling:

¾ cup heavy cream

5 ounces dark chocolate, finely chopped

1 tablespoon unsalted butter, diced, plus extra for greasing

1 Grease a 9 x 13-inch jelly roll pan with butter and line with baking parchment.

2 To make the sponge, break up the chocolate and put it in a heatproof bowl. Set the bowl over a pan of gently simmering water, making sure the water isn't touching the base of the bowl, and leave until melted. Turn off the heat and allow to cool slightly.

3 Meanwhile, put the egg yolks and sugar in a large bowl and whisk until pale and creamy. Pour in the melted chocolate and mix it in gently. In a separate large bowl, whisk the egg whites until they form stiff peaks. Stir a third of the whites into the chocolate mixture to loosen it, then fold in the rest with a large metal spoon.

4 Pour the mixture into the prepared pan, smooth the top and place in an oven preheated to 350°F. Bake for 20 minutes or until firm to the touch. Remove the pan from the oven and leave to stand for a few minutes, then place a damp cloth, such as a tea towel, over the top and leave the cake in the pan to cool completely.

5 Meanwhile, make the filling. Put the cream into a pan and bring to a boil. Put the chopped chocolate into a heatproof bowl and pour the hot cream over it. Leave for a minute and then stir gently to melt the chocolate. Add the butter and stir again. Leave to cool, then place in the fridge for an hour, until thickened.

6 When ready to assemble the roulade, dust a sheet of baking parchment with cocoa powder. Turn the cake out of the pan on to the paper. Peel off the parchment from the base of the cake and spread the chocolate ganache over it, leaving a 3/4-inch border all round. Scatter the cherries over.

7 Whip the heavy cream with the confectioner's sugar until quite stiff and spread it in a thin layer all over the chocolate ganache and cherries. Now roll up the cake, using the baking parchment to help lift and roll it, ending up with the seam underneath. Roll it up quite tightly in the baking parchment and leave it in the fridge for at least 4 hours.

8 Saw through the paper with a sharp serrated knife to trim off the ends of the cake, then carefully unwrap the cake. Slide it on to a serving platter and dust with confectioner's sugar. It's very good served with Crème Anglaise (see pages 222–223).

QUICK BREADS
and
BREADS

Quick breads are ideal for the baker in a hurry. Yeast-free, they cover the whole spectrum from scones to potato bread, muffins and cobblers. Breads that rely on yeast to rise might sound time consuming to make but in fact they need very little hands-on attention. If you like, you can make the dough the night before, leave it in the fridge to rise and then shape and bake it in the morning.

Effie Morrison from Scotland taught me the secret of keeping scones light. When I watched her make them, it was as if she wasn't mixing the dough at all, but simply aerating it with the tips of her fingers.

SCONES

MAKES 8–10

11 ounces self-rising flour

1 teaspoon baking powder

1 heaped teaspoon cream of tartar

a pinch of salt

3½ tablespoons unsalted butter, diced

2 ounces superfine sugar

1 egg

½ cup milk, plus extra for brushing

1 Sift the flour, baking powder, cream of tartar and salt into a large bowl.

2 Rub in the butter with your fingertips until the mixture resembles breadcrumbs.

3 Then stir in the sugar.

4 Lightly beat the egg and milk together in a glass or small bowl.

5 Make a well in the center of the flour and pour in the egg mixture – it's a good idea to hold a little back in case the dough is too wet.

6 Mix with a round-bladed knife or a fork.

7 Then bring together very lightly with your hands, adding the rest of the egg mixture if necessary. The dough should be very soft but not wet.

8 Put the dough on a lightly floured work surface.

9 Pat out the dough gently with your hands to about ¾ inch thick.

10 Cut out rounds with a 2½-inch pastry cutter, or cut into squares with a sharp knife.

11 Transfer the scones to a greased baking sheet.

12 Brush the scones with milk and place in an oven preheated to 400°F. Bake for 12 minutes or until golden brown.

QUICK BREADS AND BREADS

scone variations

Fruit Scones – follow the recipe on pages 258–259, stirring in 5 ounces mixed raisins and golden raisins after adding the sugar.

Cheese Scones – follow the recipe on pages 258–259, omitting the sugar and stirring in 5 ounces finely grated Gruyère cheese, a good pinch of cayenne pepper and 5 tablespoons of finely chopped chives instead. Roll or pat the dough out on a lightly floured work surface into a circle about ¾ inch thick. Cut into 8 wedges, put them on a greased baking sheet and bake at 400°F for 15–20 minutes, until golden brown.

Walnut Scones – follow the recipe on pages 258–259, stirring in 3½ tablespoons of finely chopped walnuts after adding the sugar.

Herb Scones – follow the recipe on pages 258–259, omitting the sugar and stirring in 5 tablespoons of chopped mixed herbs instead.

TIPS AND IDEAS

■ Quick breads involve no yeast and no kneading and many of them are indeed very quick to cook. Some can even be fried, such as Irish Potato Bread (see page 262).

■ A light touch gives a light result when making scones. The heavier the dough, the firmer the scone will be, so handle it as little as possible. Don't knead it until smooth, just bring it together quickly and lightly – don't worry if it feels slightly lumpy.

■ The quickest and easiest way to cut out scones is to roll or pat out the dough and then cut it into squares or triangles with a floured knife. For round scones, use a cutter, but you will need to bring the trimmings back together. I pile them up and lightly roll or pat them out again.

■ Scones can be glazed with milk, or with beaten egg for a richer glaze. Sprinkle sweet scones with sugar after glazing, if you like.

■ Scones are best eaten fresh, but they do freeze well.

■ I am a traditionalist when it comes to sweet scones – the only way to eat them is with strawberry jam and a large dollop of clotted cream!

■ You can make a quick cobbler topping by dropping your usual savory scone mixture on top of a cooked stew, or sweet scone mixture on top of cooked fruit, and baking in the oven at 400°F until risen and browned.

IRISH POTATO BREAD

I was introduced to this recipe by my friend, Keith Fleming, from Ireland. He is the most amazing baker and taught me to appreciate this marvelous bread.

Makes 8

1¼ pounds potatoes, peeled and cut into chunks

3 tablespoons very soft butter

1 teaspoon salt

3.5 ounces all-purpose flour

1 Cook the potatoes in boiling salted water until tender, then drain thoroughly. Leave in the colander for a few minutes to steam off excess moisture. Mash the potatoes until smooth (or push them through a potato ricer or sieve), put them in a bowl and add the soft butter and salt. Sift the flour over and work it in until you have a pliable dough; you may need to add a little more flour if the mixture is too sticky.

2 Turn the dough out onto a floured work surface and roll out into a 10-inch square, about 1/4 inch thick. Cut into 8 rectangles. If you have time, put them in the fridge, covered, for 2 hours, but you can cook them straight away if necessary.

3 Heat a dry, heavy-bottomed frying pan or a flat griddle over a moderate heat. Test to see if it is hot enough by dusting with a little flour – when it turns golden, the pan is ready. Add the potato bread and cook over a fairly low heat for 5–10 minutes, turning once, until browned on both sides and cooked through. They are also very good fried in a little oil or goose fat.

SODA BREAD

If you don't have any buttermilk in the house, you can sour some milk and use that instead. Simply add 2½ teaspoons of white wine vinegar to 1 cup whole milk and leave overnight.

Makes 1 loaf

1 pound all-purpose flour

1 teaspoon salt

2½ teaspoons baking soda

about 2 cups buttermilk

1 teaspoon sunflower oil

1 Put the flour into a large bowl, add the salt and baking soda and mix well. Add 2 cups buttermilk and the sunflower oil and mix lightly with a wooden spoon, adding a little more buttermilk if the mixture is too dry.

2 Turn out the dough on to a lightly floured surface and shape into a ball. Put the loaf on a floured baking tray and make a cross in the top with a knife, dipping it in flour first so it doesn't stick.

3 Place in an oven preheated to 425°F and bake for 25 minutes, then reduce the temperature to 280°F. Bake for another 25 minutes or until the loaf sounds hollow when tapped on the base. Transfer to a wire rack and leave to cool. This bread is best eaten on the day of baking.

soda bread variation

Soda Bread Scones – for 4 scones, make half the quantity of dough above. Turn out onto a well-floured surface, push down with your hands until ½ inch thick, cut into 4 and place on a heated flat griddle. Bake over a low heat for up to 5 minutes on each side, until golden brown.

BEEF STEW WITH SCONE TOPPING

This is such a warming dish. Make sure the meat is really tender before you add the scone topping, which finishes it off perfectly.

Serves 4

2 ounces all-purpose flour, seasoned with salt and pepper

1¾ pounds shin of beef, cut into 1-inch cubes

2½ tablespoons olive oil

1 onion, cut into ½-inch dice

1 carrot, cut into ½-inch dice

2 celery stalks, sliced

3 anchovy fillets in oil, drained and chopped

1 cup red wine

about 3 cups beef stock (see page 34)

sea salt and black pepper

For the scone topping:

5 ounces self-rising flour

½ teaspoon baking powder

½ heaped teaspoon cream of tartar

a pinch of salt

2 tablespoons unsalted butter, diced

1 egg yolk, lightly beaten

4 tablespoons milk, plus extra for brushing

1 Spread the seasoned flour out on a large plate and roll the beef in it. Heat the olive oil in a large frying pan and brown the beef in batches, transferring it to a casserole as it is done. Reduce the heat under the pan, add a little more oil if necessary and cook the onion, carrot and celery in it until softened. Add the anchovies and stir until they disintegrate, then add this mixture to the casserole.

2 Pour the wine into the frying pan and bring to a boil, scraping the bottom of the pan with a wooden spoon to deglaze it. Simmer until reduced by a third, then pour the wine over the meat and add enough stock just to cover the meat. Season with salt and pepper and bring to a boil. Cover the casserole, transfer to an oven preheated to 300°F and cook for 2 hours.

3 Meanwhile, prepare the scone topping. Sift the flour, baking powder, cream of tartar and salt into a bowl and then rub in the butter with your fingertips. Stir in the beaten egg yolk and the milk, then divide the mixture into 4 and shape into flattened rounds.

4 Raise the oven temperature to 350°F. Put the scones on top of the stew and return it to the oven without the lid. Cook for 20 minutes, until the scones are well risen and browned.

CORNBREAD

This is a classic American quick bread. It makes a lovely accompaniment to Chili con Carne (see page 183).

Makes 20

11 ounces all-purpose flour

11 ounces cornmeal

2.5 ounces superfine sugar

1 teaspoon salt

1 tablespoon baking powder

6 tablespoons unsalted butter, melted, plus extra for greasing

¾ cup buttermilk

1¼ cups whole milk

2 eggs

1 Put the flour, cornmeal, sugar, salt and baking powder into a large bowl and mix well. Put all the remaining ingredients into a large glass, lightly whisk together, then pour into the bowl. Stir together to form a soft batter – be careful not to overwork it.

2 Pour the mixture into a greased 9-inch square pan and place in an oven preheated to 400°F. Bake for 20–25 minutes, until the cornbread is well risen and a skewer inserted in the center comes out clean. Leave to cool, then cut into squares to serve.

BLUEBERRY MUFFINS

Another American classic and always very popular with children.

Makes 12

5 ounces self-rising flour

5 ounces all-purpose flour

2½ teaspoons baking powder

4.5 ounces superfine sugar

3 eggs

⅔ cup milk

1 teaspoon vanilla extract

6 tablespoons unsalted butter, melted

5 ounces blueberries

1 Line a muffin tin with cupcake liners (they tend to pop out before they are filled, so I put a tiny bit of butter inside the tin so the cases will stick).

2 Sift the flours and baking powder into a large bowl and stir in the sugar. In a glass, lightly whisk the eggs, milk, vanilla extract and melted butter together, then add to the flour. Stir together lightly until just combined (do not overmix, as this will make the muffins tough). Quickly fold in the blueberries.

3 Spoon the mixture into the cupcake liners. Bake in an oven preheated to 400°F for 18–20 minutes, until well risen and golden brown, then remove. Transfer to a wire rack to cool.

muffin variations

Banana Muffins – replace the blueberries with 2 ripe bananas mashed with 1 teaspoon ground cinnamon and reduce the milk to ½ cup.

Lemon Muffins – omit the blueberries. Substitute lemon juice for ¼ cup of the milk and add the grated zest of 2 lemons.

APPLE AND BLACKBERRY COBBLER

The cobbler topping contains buttermilk, which makes a wonderfully light, tender dough. It complements fruit perfectly and is well worth trying as an alternative to the more usual crumble.

Serves 6

2 ounces all-purpose flour

2 teaspoons chilled unsalted butter, plus extra to grease the dish

2.5 ounces superfine sugar

2½ teaspoons cornstarch

6 large cooking apples, peeled, cored and sliced

juice and grated zest of 1 large orange

2½ tablespoons lemon juice

grated zest of 1 lemon

9 ounces blackberries

For the cobbler topping:

5 ounces all-purpose flour

2½ teaspoons baking powder

½ teaspoon salt

1.5 ounces superfine sugar

3½ tablespoons unsalted butter, diced

½ cup buttermilk, plus extra milk if needed

1 teaspoon vanilla extract

For the glaze:

1 tablespoon heavy cream

2½ teaspoons sugar

1 teaspoon ground cinnamon

1 Put the flour into a large bowl and rub in the chilled butter. Stir in the sugar and cornstarch, then add the apples, orange and lemon juice, orange and lemon zest and the blackberries and toss well. Put into a buttered shallow gratin dish.

2 To make the cobbler topping, sift the flour, baking powder and salt into a large bowl, stir in the sugar, then rub in the butter with your fingertips, until the mixture resembles breadcrumbs. Add the buttermilk and vanilla extract and mix to create a soft dough – add a little milk or extra buttermilk if needed. Drop spoonfuls of the dough onto the fruit.

3 Mix all the ingredients for the glaze together in a small bowl. Brush the glaze on to the dough and then place in an oven preheated to 400°F. Bake for about 35 minutes, until the cobbler topping is risen and browned, turning the oven down to 350°F after about 25 minutes if it browns too quickly. Serve with ice cream.

FAT RASCALS

You find these in bakeries all over Yorkshire but I've never seen them anywhere else. They are like a cross between a scone and a rock cake (a small fruitcake) but tend to be slightly richer than either.

Makes 8

12 ounces all-purpose flour

1½ rounded teaspoons baking powder

3½ teaspoons ground cinnamon

3.5 ounces unsalted butter, diced, plus extra for greasing

3.5 ounces superfine sugar

3 ounces raisins

2 ounces golden raisins

2 ounces diced candied orange peel

grated zest of 2 lemons

⅓ cup sour cream

1 egg

¼ cup milk

To decorate:

1 egg, lightly beaten

8 glacé (candied) cherries

24 slivered almonds

1 Sift the flour, baking powder and cinnamon into a large bowl. Add the butter and rub it in with your fingertips until the mixture resembles breadcrumbs. Stir in the sugar, raisins, golden raisins, candied peel and lemon zest.

2 Lightly beat the sour cream, egg and milk together, add to the mixture and stir together to form a soft dough. Turn out on to a floured board and roll out to about 3/4 inch thick. Cut into rounds about 3 inches in diameter, re-rolling the trimmings as necessary.

3 Transfer to a greased baking sheet, spacing them well apart, brush with the beaten egg and then decorate each one with 2 cherry halves and 3 slivered almonds. Traditionally they are used to make a face: cherries for eyes and the almonds for teeth.

4 Put the fat rascals in an oven preheated to 400°F and bake for 15–18 minutes, until golden brown. Remove from the oven and leave to cool on a wire rack. The fat rascals will keep for 2–3 days.

WHOLE WHEAT LOAF

This traditional stoneground whole wheat loaf is quite dense in texture. If you prefer a lighter bread, try the variation below, which includes some white flour. The key to making this loaf is to knead it for a little longer than usual to get the gluten in the flour working.

Makes 1 large or 2 small loaves

23 ounces whole wheat bread flour

1 ounce fresh yeast (or a 0.25-ounce package of active dry yeast)

2 cups tepid water

0.35 ounces fine sea salt

1 Put the flour into a large bowl, crumble in the yeast (or stir in the dry yeast) and mix well. Add the tepid water and stir to make a rough dough. If it feels too dry or firm, add a little more water until you have a lovely soft, pliable dough.

2 Turn the dough out onto a work surface. Knead the dough by holding it down at the front with the fingers of one hand and pushing the rest of it with the palm of your other hand to stretch it, then rolling the dough up and giving it a quarter turn. Your hands will become sticky, so dip them regularly into a bowl of flour, clapping your hands together to shake off the excess. Knead the dough in this way for about 7 minutes, until it begins to feel elastic, then sprinkle on the salt and keep stretching and kneading for another 7 minutes to work the gluten and achieve a good, pliable dough. After adding the salt, the dough will feel slightly wetter, as the salt draws the water out. Don't worry; just flour your hands as necessary.

3 Shape the dough into a ball and put it into a large floured bowl. Cover with plastic wrap and leave to rise at room temperature for about 2 hours, until it has doubled in size.

4 Punch the dough down once or twice with your fist to knock the air out. Knead briefly, then shape it into an oval to fit an oiled 2-pound loaf pan (or into 2 ovals to fit 2 smaller pans). Leave to rise again, uncovered, for another 1 1/2 hours.

5 Brush the top of the loaf with water and place in an oven preheated to 425°F. Bake for 20 minutes, then reduce the temperature to 350°F and bake for another 20–25 minutes. Remove the loaf from the oven, tip it out of the pan and tap the base with your knuckles; if it sounds hollow, the loaf is done. If not, put it back in the oven upside down for about 10 minutes. Leave on a wire rack to cool.

whole wheat loaf variations

Light Whole Wheat Bread – follow the recipe above, using 14 ounces white bread flour and 9 ounces whole wheat bread flour. This loaf will take only 1–1½ hours for the first rise and 1 hour after punching down.

■ After brushing the top of the loaf with water, sprinkle with oats or seeds – poppy, sesame and sunflower seeds are all delicious options.

How to knead dough

Some people think of kneading as a pummeling action but in fact the most effective way to knead bread is to keep stretching it out and then rolling it up, in order to work the gluten. Here is how to do it.

1 Hold the dough down at the front with the fingers of one hand and push the rest of it with the palm of your other hand to stretch it.

2 Then roll the dough up.

3 Give the dough a quarter turn and repeat steps 1–3 as you continue to knead.

TIPS AND IDEAS

■ Good flour is essential when making bread. Try to find stoneground organic flour – none of the nutrients have been removed and it will have a wonderful flavor.

■ Salt delays the activation of the yeast, so I prefer to add it to the dough halfway through the kneading process.

■ When kneading, flour your hands, not the work surface, so you don't incorporate too much flour into the dough. Work as quickly as possible to prevent the dough sticking.

■ You can adapt the rising (also known as 'proofing') time to suit you by controling the temperature at which the dough rises – if you leave it in the fridge overnight, for example, it will rise slowly and you can bake fresh bread for breakfast. A warm place will speed up the rising time, but make sure it's not too warm or you will kill the yeast. A slow rise gives a slightly better flavor.

■ Bread freezes like a dream. It is worth baking a couple of batches at once, so you have plenty ready to go. Wrap it well in a plastic bag before freezing.

■ In my opinion, bread machines do not produce good bread. They create a lovely smell and are undoubtedly useful to some people, but they don't knead the dough properly and therefore cannot produce the same quality as bread made by hand.

WHITE LOAF

This loaf contains butter, which means its shelf life is slightly longer than usual. A good organic flour is the way to go for an outstanding flavor.

Makes 1 large loaf

23 ounces white bread flour

3½ tablespoons cold unsalted butter, diced, plus extra for greasing

0.5 ounce fresh yeast (or a 0.25-ounce package of active dry yeast)

2 cups tepid water

0.35 ounces fine sea salt

1 Put the flour into a large bowl and rub in the butter with your fingertips. Crumble in the fresh yeast (or stir in the dried yeast) and mix well. Add the water and stir to make a rough dough. If it feels too dry or firm, add a little more water until you have a lovely soft, pliable dough.

2 Turn the dough out on to a work surface and knead for about 10 minutes, following the instructions on page 270. Sprinkle over the salt and knead for 5 minutes longer. Shape the dough into a ball, return it to the bowl and cover with plastic wrap. Leave to rise at room temperature for 1–1 1/2 hours, until it has doubled in size.

3 Punch down the dough then shape it into an oval to fit a greased 2-pound loaf pan. Leave to rise again, uncovered, for about 1 hour, until doubled in size.

4 Place the loaf in an oven preheated to 425°F and bake for 20 minutes. Turn the heat down to 350°F and bake for a further 25 minutes, until the loaf sounds hollow when tapped underneath. Leave on a wire rack to cool.

HERB ROLLS

I have included a little rye flour in these rolls to give them extra body. Be generous with the herbs, particularly in the summer if you have them growing in your garden.

Makes 20

1 pound white bread flour

7 ounces rye flour

1 ounce fresh yeast (or a 0.25-ounce package of active dry yeast)

2½ tablespoons unsalted butter, melted

1 egg yolk

1⅔ cups tepid water

0.35 ounce fine sea salt

1 ounce chopped mixed herbs (dill and thyme are good)

1 Put the flours into a large bowl and make a well in the center. Crumble in the fresh yeast (or stir in the dried yeast), then add the melted butter, egg yolk and water. Stir to make a rough dough, adding a little more water if it feels too firm.

2 Turn the dough out on to a work surface and knead for about 10 minutes, following the instructions on page 270. Sprinkle over the salt and knead for about 5 minutes longer. Shape the dough into a ball, return it to the bowl and cover with plastic wrap. Leave to rise at room temperature for about 2 hours, until it has doubled in size.

3 Punch down the dough and gently knead in the fresh herbs. Divide it into 20 equal pieces and shape into balls. Arrange them well spaced out on 1 or 2 floured baking sheets and leave to rise, uncovered, for 30 minutes or until doubled in size.

4 Place in an oven preheated to 400°F and bake for 15 minutes, until the rolls sound hollow when tapped underneath.

WALNUT AND RYE BREAD

This makes an interesting alternative to a standard brown loaf.

Makes 3 small loaves

14 ounces white bread flour

9 ounces rye flour

1 ounce fresh yeast (or a 0.25-ounce package of active dry yeast)

2 cups tepid water

2½ tablespoons walnut oil

0.35 ounce fine sea salt

a large handful of walnuts, chopped

1 Put the flours into a large bowl and crumble in the fresh yeast (or stir in the dried yeast). Add the water and walnut oil and stir to make a rough dough, adding a little more water if it feels too dry.

2 Turn the dough out on to a work surface and knead for about 10 minutes, following the instructions on page 270. Sprinkle over the salt and knead for another 5 minutes, adding the walnuts towards the end of the process. Shape the dough into a ball, return it to the bowl and cover with plastic wrap. Leave to rise at room temperature for about 1 hour, until it has doubled in size.

3 Punch down the dough, then divide it into 3 equal pieces. Shape them into long sticks, place on a floured baking sheet and leave to rise, uncovered, until they have doubled in size.

4 Put the loaves into an oven preheated to 425°F and bake for 10 minutes, then turn down the heat to 350°F and bake for another 20–30 minutes, until the loaves sound hollow when tapped underneath. Transfer to a wire rack to cool.

PITA BREAD

There is absolutely no comparison between purchased and home-made pita bread. Try serving with really good hummus.

Makes 10

1¼ pounds white bread flour

1 ounce fresh yeast (or a 0.25-ounce package of active dry yeast)

1⅔ cups tepid water

⅛ cup olive oil, plus extra for sprinkling

1 ounce superfine sugar

0.35 ounce fine sea salt, plus extra for sprinkling

1 Put the flour into a large bowl and crumble in the fresh yeast (or stir in the dried yeast). Mix well, then add the water, olive oil and sugar and stir to make a rough dough.

2 Turn the dough out on to a work surface and knead for about 10 minutes, following the instructions on page 270. Add the salt and continue kneading for about 5 minutes, until the dough is supple and pliable. Return it to the bowl, cover with plastic wrap and leave to rise for about 1 hour, until it has doubled in size.

3 Punch down the dough and divide it into 10 pieces. Flatten each one to about 1/4 inch thick with the palm of your hand or with a rolling pin. Lay them on a floured cloth, sprinkle with flour and cover with another cloth. Leave to rise for just 10 minutes. Meanwhile, put a lightly oiled baking sheet in the oven to heat at 425°F.

4 Slide the pita breads onto the baking sheet (you'll probably need to cook them in batches), sprinkle with a little olive oil and sea salt and bake for 8–10 minutes, until they are slightly puffy.

PIZZA

All children love to make pizza — it's a wonderful way to get them involved with fresh ingredients. If they are too young to join in the baking, let them choose their toppings and decorate their own pizza.

Makes 1 large or 2 small pizzas

9 ounces white bread flour

0.5 ounce fresh yeast (or ½ a package of active dry yeast)

½ cup tepid water

3½ tablespoons milk

1 tablespoon olive oil

a pinch of salt

For the tomato sauce:

2½ tablespoons olive oil

1 small onion, finely chopped

2 garlic cloves, finely chopped

18 ounces tomatoes, skinned, deseeded and chopped (see page 135)

½ teaspoon sugar

1 tablespoon tomato paste

1 tablespoon chopped basil

sea salt and black pepper

Toppings – choose from the following:

- Mozzarella, ricotta, Parmesan, goat cheese
- Cooked artichoke hearts, fried eggplant or mushroom slices, thinly sliced raw red pepper
- Olives, chile, arugula (scatter arugula on the pizza when it comes out of the oven)
- Basil, thyme, marjoram, sage, rosemary
- Mussels or anchovies
- Mortadella, salami, prosciutto

1 Put the flour into a bowl and crumble in the fresh yeast (or stir in the dried yeast). Add the water, milk and olive oil and stir together to make a rough dough, adding a little more water if it feels too dry.

2 Turn the dough out on to a work surface and knead for 5 minutes, following the instructions on page 270. Sprinkle the salt over and knead for 5 minutes longer, then return the dough to the bowl, cover with plastic wrap and leave at room temperature for about an hour, until doubled in size.

3 Meanwhile, make the tomato sauce. Heat the olive oil in a saucepan, add the onion and garlic and cook gently until softened. Add the chopped tomatoes and sugar and cook, covered, for about 10 minutes, until the tomatoes have given off their juices. Uncover the pan and continue cooking for about 20 minutes, until the liquid has evaporated and the sauce is thick. Stir in the tomato paste and basil, cook for a couple of minutes longer and season to taste.

4 Put a large baking sheet into the oven to heat at 425°F. Punch down the risen dough and cut it in half if you want to make 2 pizzas, or leave it whole for 1 big pizza. Roll it out on a floured surface into a round about 1/4 inch thick and place on a baking sheet. Spread the tomato sauce over the dough and add the toppings of your choice.

5 Place the baking sheet with the pizza on it directly on to the hot baking sheet in the oven and bake for 12–15 minutes, until the top of the pizza is bubbling and the base is golden around the edges.

FRENCH BREAD WITH FLAVORINGS

This is slightly heavier than a standard baguette but is the best bread ever. You can add any flavor you like to it — but be sure to eat it on the day it is made, or refresh it in a hot oven.

Makes 4 loaves

30 ounces white bread flour

1 ounce fresh yeast (or 1½ packages of active dry yeast)

2⅓ cups tepid water

0.5 ounce fine sea salt

First-proof flavorings:

■ Canadian bacon and onion – finely dice 6 bacon slices and cook them in a little oil, then remove from the pan and put to one side. Gently fry 2 finely diced onions until soft, then add to the bacon and leave to cool.

■ Black olives – 7 finely chopped tablespoons.

■ Red pepper – drain a bottle of red peppers in oil and purée.

Second-proof flavorings:

■ Poppy seeds

■ Sesame seeds

■ Thyme

■ Saffron

■ Sunflower seeds

■ Oats

1 Put the flour into a large bowl and crumble in the fresh yeast (or stir in the dried yeast). Add the water and stir to make a rough dough, adding a little more water if it feels too dry.

2 Turn the dough out on to a work surface and knead for 10 minutes, following the instructions on page 270. Sprinkle on the salt and knead for another 5 minutes, then gently knead in any first-proof flavorings you would like to use. Shape the dough into a ball, put it in a floured bowl and cover with plastic wrap. Leave to rise at room temperature for about 1 hour, until it has doubled in size.

3 Punch down the dough and divide it into 4, then roll out each piece into a long stick. Place the sticks on a floured baking sheet, leaving plenty of space between them, and make several slashes across the top of each loaf with a sharp knife. Leave to rise for 30 minutes or until doubled in size.

4 If you are adding any second-proof flavorings, brush the tops of the loaves with water and scatter the flavorings over. Place in an oven preheated to 425°F and bake for 10 minutes. Reduce the heat to 300°F and bake for a further 25 minutes, until the bread sounds hollow when tapped underneath.

FOCACCIA

It might seem like there is a lot of oil in this rustic Italian bread but it means that the dough effectively 'fries' in the oven, giving a gorgeously crisp exterior and a beautiful golden color. I've suggested a couple of toppings below, but you can try anything that takes your fancy. Focaccia is usually served cut into squares for dipping in really good olive oil. I honestly don't think anything could be more delicious.

Makes 2 loaves

1¼ pounds white bread flour

0.5 ounce fresh yeast (or a 0.25-ounce package of active dry yeast)

1⅔ cups water, at room temperature

0.35 ounce fine sea salt

about ⅓ cup olive oil

For the topping:

▪ crushed garlic, tiny sprigs of rosemary and sea salt

or:

▪ finely sliced red onion, chopped mint and/or cilantro, cumin seeds and sea salt

1 Put the flour into a large bowl, make a well in the center and crumble in the fresh yeast (or stir in the dried yeast). Add the water and mix well to form a dough, adding a little more water if it feels too dry.

2 Turn the dough out on to a work surface and knead for about 10 minutes, following the instructions on page 270. Sprinkle the salt over and knead for another 5 minutes.

3 Shape the dough into a ball, return it to the bowl and brush it with olive oil. Cover loosely with plastic wrap and leave to rise for 1–1 1/2 hours, until it has doubled in size.

4 Punch down the risen dough and divide it in half. Pour some of the olive oil into two square 8-inch cake pans so it covers the bottom in a layer about 1/8 inch deep. Stretch the pieces of dough out to fit the pans, then place one in each pan, pressing it well into the sides. Sprinkle more olive oil over the dough and then, using your fingertips, press dents all over the top, pushing right to the bottom so the oil seeps through the dough. Add your chosen topping and press it into the dough to help the flavors to penetrate. Then sprinkle more oil over the surface, if desired, and finish by scattering some sea salt on top.

5 Leave the loaves to rise for 1 hour or until doubled in size. Place in an oven preheated to 425°F and bake for 20 minutes or until golden. Turn the focaccia out of the pans and leave to cool on a wire rack.

FOUGASSE

Fougasse is a kind of Provençal flat bread, made with olive oil and often slashed before baking to create slits in the loaf. It can be flavored with piquant ingredients, such as anchovies, olives, herbs and cheese. I like to make three small loaves and use a different flavoring for each one. This bread is best eaten on the day it is made but it does freeze very well.

Makes 3 small loaves

23 ounces white bread flour

1 ounce fresh yeast (or a 0.25-ounce package of active dry yeast)

2 cups tepid water

3½ tablespoons olive oil, plus extra for sprinkling

0.5 ounce fine sea salt

To flavor the dough:

5 anchovies, chopped

2½ rounded tablespoons roughly chopped black olives

1 rounded tablespoon finely chopped rosemary

1 Put the flour into a bowl, crumble in the fresh yeast (or stir in the dried yeast) and mix well. Add the water and oil and mix to form a dough, adding a little more water if it feels too dry.

2 Turn the dough out on to a work surface and knead for 10 minutes, following the instructions on page 270. Sprinkle the salt on and knead for another 5 minutes, until smooth and elastic.

3 Shape the dough into a ball, place it in a lightly floured bowl, then cover loosely with plastic wrap and leave to rise for about an hour, until it has doubled in size.

4 Punch down the dough and divide it into 3 pieces. Add the anchovies to one piece and gently knead them in. Add the olives and the rosemary to the remaining pieces in the same way.

5 Roll out each piece into an oval approximately 1/4 inch thick. Using a sharp knife, cut 3 parallel slits at an angle across the center of each loaf, being sure to cut right through the dough. Stretch each loaf slightly so that the slits open up a little and it looks like a ladder. Put each one on a baking sheet and leave to rise for 30 minutes.

6 Sprinkle the loaves with olive oil, place in an oven preheated to 425°F and bake for 15–20 minutes, until golden brown. Leave to cool on a wire rack.

BEER BREAD

Old Peculier beer is made in my local town and is the one I always use for this bread. If you can't get it, you need to use a really strong, dark beer.

Makes 1 loaf

1½ pounds white bread flour

1 ounce fresh yeast (or a 0.25-ounce package of active dry yeast)

2 cups dark beer, preferably Old Peculier

⅓ cup honey

0.35 ounce fine sea salt

1 Put the flour into a large bowl, crumble in the fresh yeast (or stir in the dried yeast) and mix well. Pour in the beer and honey and stir to make a rough dough. Turn the dough out on to a work surface and knead for about 10 minutes, following the instructions on page 270. Sprinkle over the salt and knead for 5 minutes longer. Shape the dough into a ball, return it to the bowl and cover with plastic wrap. Leave to rise at room temperature for about 1 hour, until it has doubled in size.

2 Punch down the dough and divide it into 6 pieces. Shape one into a ball and the other 5 into ovals. Press these on to the round shape so it looks like a star. Transfer to a floured baking sheet and leave to rise again for 30–40 minutes, until doubled in size.

3 Place the loaf in an oven preheated to 425°F and bake for 20–25 minutes, until it sounds hollow when tapped underneath. Transfer to a wire rack and leave to cool.

RICH WHITE LOAF

You can divide the dough into three strands after the first rising and shape it into a plait, if you prefer.

Makes 1 large loaf

23 ounces white bread flour

1 ounce fresh yeast (or a 0.25-ounce package of active dry yeast)

6 tablespoons unsalted butter, diced

1½ cups milk

1 teaspoon sugar

1 egg, beaten

0.35 ounce fine sea salt

1 egg yolk mixed with 1 tablespoon water, to glaze

1 Put the flour into a large mixing bowl, crumble in the fresh yeast (or stir in the dried yeast) and mix well. Gently heat the butter, milk and sugar in a pan until the butter has melted. Allow to cool to body temperature, then stir in the egg. Add to the flour and stir until a soft dough is formed. Turn it out on to a work surface and knead for 10 minutes, following the instructions on page 270. Sprinkle with salt and continue to knead for 5 minutes, until smooth and elastic. Return the dough to the bowl, cover and leave for 1–1 1/2 hours, until doubled in size.

2 Punch down the dough and knead lightly. Shape into an oval and place in a greased 2-pound loaf pan, then leave to rise for about 1 hour, until doubled in size. Brush with the egg glaze and place in an oven preheated to 400°F. Bake for 30 minutes, then reduce the oven to 300°F and bake for 15 minutes longer, until the loaf sounds hollow when tapped underneath. Cool on a wire rack.

> *rich white loaf variation*
>
> **Saffron Bread** – add a good pinch of saffron strands to the warm milk.

HOT CROSS BUNS

These are so much better than the ones sold in the shops, and you can adjust the amount of spice to suit your taste. If you don't want to make the crosses, simply mark a cross on top of each bun with a knife.

Makes 10–12

5 ounces mixed raisins and golden raisins

18 ounces white bread flour

2½ teaspoons ground pie spice

2½ teaspoons ground cinnamon

3½ tablespoons unsalted butter, diced

0.5 ounce fresh yeast (or a 0.25-ounce package of active dry yeast)

1.5 ounces superfine sugar

¾ cup milk

1 egg

0.35 ounce fine sea salt

For the crosses:

2½ tablespoons all-purpose flour

½ tablespoon superfine sugar

a small pinch of baking soda

1 tablespoon vegetable oil

1 tablespoon water

For the glaze:

3.5 ounces white sugar

3½ tablespoons water

1 Put the raisins and golden raisins in a bowl, cover with boiling water and leave to soak for 15 minutes while you start your dough.

2 Put the flour and spices into a large bowl and rub in the butter with your fingertips. Crumble in the fresh yeast (or stir in the dried yeast). Add the sugar, milk and egg and mix to a soft dough. Turn the dough out on to a work surface and knead for about 10 minutes, following the instructions on page 270. Sprinkle the salt over and knead for another 5 minutes. Drain the fruit and gently knead it into the dough. Shape the dough into a ball, return it to the bowl and cover with plastic wrap. Leave to rise at room temperature for about 1 hour, until it has doubled in size.

3 Punch down the dough, knead lightly, then cut it into 10–12 equal pieces and shape them into balls. Place them well spaced out on 1 or 2 floured baking sheets and leave to rise for 30 minutes or until doubled in size.

4 Meanwhile, make the paste for the crosses: put the flour, sugar and baking soda into a bowl and stir in the vegetable oil and water. Put the paste into a piping bag fitted with a small nozzle.

5 Using the back of a knife, mark a cross on each risen bun, then pipe the paste on to it. Place the buns in an oven preheated to 350°F and bake for 15–20 minutes. Meanwhile, make the glaze. Put the sugar and water in a small pan and heat gently, stirring to dissolve the sugar. Bring to a boil and boil for 2 minutes or until it is syrupy; it should register 230°F on a candy thermometer, if you have one.

6 When the buns are golden brown, remove from the oven and brush with the hot sugar glaze. Put them on to a wire rack to cool.

INDEX

CONVERSION CHARTS

OVEN TEMPERATURES

°F	°C	°C (fan)	Gas mark
225°F	110°C	90°C	¼
250°F	120°C	100°C	½
275°F	140°C	120°C	1
300°F	150°C	130°C	2
325°F	160°C	140°C	3
350°F	180°C	160°C	4
375°F	190°C	170°C	5
400°F	200°C	180°C	6
425°F	220°C	200°C	7
450°F	230°C	210°C	8
475°F	240°C	220°C	9

SPOONS

Standard level spoon measurements are used in all recipes.

WEIGHTS

¼oz	5g
½oz	15g
¾oz	20g
1oz	25g
2oz	50g
3oz	75g
4oz	125g
5oz	150g
6oz	175g
7oz	200g
8oz	250g
9oz	275g
10oz	300g
11oz	325g
12oz	375g
13oz	400g
14oz	425g
15oz	475g
1lb	500g
1¼lb	625g
1½lb	750g
1¾lb	875g
2lb	1kg
2½lb	1.25kg
3lb	1.5kg
3½lb	1.75kg
4lb	2kg

VOLUME

½ fl oz	15ml
1 fl oz	25ml
2 fl oz	50ml
3 fl oz	75ml
3½ fl oz	100 ml
4 fl oz	125ml
¼ pint	150ml
6 fl oz	175ml
7 fl oz	200ml
8 fl oz	250ml
9 fl oz	275ml
½ pint	300ml
11 fl oz	325ml
12 fl oz	350ml
13 fl oz	375ml
400ml	14 fl oz
¾ pint	450ml
16 fl oz	475ml
17 fl oz	500ml
18 fl oz	575ml
1 pint	600ml
1¼ pints	750ml
1½ pints	900ml
1¾ pints	1 litre
2 pints	1.2 litres
2½ pints	1.5 litres
3 pints	1.8 litres
3½ pints	2 litres
4 pints	2.5 litres

MEASUREMENTS

⅛ inch	2.5mm
¼ inch	5mm
½ inch	1cm
¾ inch	2cm
1 inch	2.5cm
2 inches	5cm
3 inches	7cm
4 inches	10cm
5 inches	12cm
6 inches	15cm
7 inches	18cm
8 inches	20cm
9 inches	23cm
10 inches	25cm
11 inches	28cm
12 inches	30cm

INDEX

**South Burlington
Public Library**

ACKNOWLEDGMENTS

This book is dedicated to my grandchildren, Freddie, Suki, Holly and Lola.

I'd like to thank many people for their help with this book. Thank you to Gillian Fieldhouse, Sue Mountgarret and Gilly Robinson for testing recipes. Thank you to Rogers Butchers and all the other shops in Masham.Thank you to Jane Middleton and Clare Churly, who both had the patience of a saint. Thank you to Belinda Wallace for the hours of deciphering. Thank you to Joy Skipper. Thank you to Cristian Barnett for the lovely photographs. Thank you to all the people at Octopus Publishing Group. And a special thank you to Stephanie Jackson for everything.

First published in Great Britain in 2011 by
Hamlyn, a division of Octopus Publishing Group Ltd
Endeavour House
189 Shaftesbury Avenue
London WC2H 8JY
www.octopusbooks.co.uk

First published in the United States in 2011 by Lyons Press

Lyons Press is an imprint of Globe Pequot Press.

ISBN 978-0-7627-7983-3

Library of Congress Cataloging-in-Publication Data is available on file.

Printed and bound in China

10 9 8 7 6 5 4 3 2 1

Note
A few recipes contain nuts and nut derivatives. Anyone with a known nut allergy must avoid these.

This book contains some dishes made with raw or lightly cooked eggs. It is prudent for more vulnerable people such as pregnant and nursing mothers, invalids, the elderly, babies and young children to avoid raw or lightly cooked eggs.